The Raj: A Time Remembered

Diary of a Voyage to India in 1917
and
Recollections of Life in
the Indian Civil Service

Donald in his Army uniform, aged 24

The Raj: A Time Remembered

Diary of a Voyage to India in 1917
and
Recollections of Life in
the Indian Civil Service

Donald MacPherson CIE

Edited by Janet Richardson

The Pentland Press Limited
Edinburgh • Cambridge • Durham • USA

© Donald MacPherson 2000

First published in 2000 by
The Pentland Press Ltd.
1 Hutton Close
South Church
Bishop Auckland
Durham

British Library Cataloguing in Publication Data.
A Catalogue record for this book is available
from the British Library.

ISBN 1 85821 756 3

Typeset by CBS, Martlesham Heath, Ipswich, Suffolk
Printed and bound by Antony Rowe Ltd.

In memory of my dear parents and a wonderful childhood in India

Janet Richardson

ACKNOWLEDGEMENTS

I would like to thank my sister Stella and my daughters Catriona and Kirsty for their encouragement and advice, and I am especially grateful to Kirsty for her help with design and publication and for the many hours she spent at the computer on my behalf.

Janet Richardson

CONTENTS

LIST OF ILLUSTRATIONS

FOREWORD

I never had the privilege of meeting Donald MacPherson, though I felt that I had. When I joined the staff of the British Museum in 1986, my senior colleague, Wladimir Zwalf, told me about him and of his continuing interest in the subcontinent born of his long period of service in British India. I vividly recall him telling me how Donald MacPherson had given a small twelfth century stone ritual plaque from Bengal decorated with the ten incarnations of Vishnu to the national collections. He also told me how, together, they had put together the wording which accompanied its donation. The plaque is still on display in the Hotung Gallery at the British Museum and the record with it states that it was 'Given by Donald MacPherson, CIE, in memory of his wife Marie, and of their happy days in India.' The beauty and poignancy of these words has always stayed with me.

Consequently, when I unexpectedly met Donald's daughter, Janet, in Darjeeling, not far from Jalpaiguri where she lived as a child, I felt that fate had indeed been kind. Both she and I were on holiday – she visiting scenes of her childhood and I relaxing after involvement with intense exhibition activities in Delhi to mark the 50th anniversary of Indian Independence. Intriguingly, a further link soon established itself in the person of her late husband Tony Richardson whom I knew quite independently from the Students' Room of my department at the Museum. In his retirement from medical practice, Tony Richardson had taken up the study of Indian religion and was writing a PhD thesis at King's College, London, concerned with the goddess Kali and her cult amongst the Thugees. I recall especially conversations on the subject of 'the divine feminine' in all its many Indian manifestations; his approach which combined medical and Indological information was enthusiastic and full of potential. It was not though until that fateful encounter with Janet Richardson on the verandah of the Windamere Hotel in 'the Place of the Thunderbolts' that I found that Tony Richardson and Donald MacPherson were related. Somehow, sitting there and looking out towards the majesty of Kanchenjunga, the extraordinary coincidence seemed only ordinary.

xiii

It was then also I learnt that, sadly, Tony had died suddenly and unexpectedly more than a year earlier.

As a member of the Indian Civil Service Donald MacPherson was one of a remarkable body of men – in those days, it was of course only men, though they were frequently accompanied by their redoubtable womenfolk. On his own patch, the ICS officer was king of all he surveyed. The ICS provided the backbone of British rule in India, with a duty to supervise impartially local land tenure, the gathering of taxes and the rule of law. In remote or rural regions of India (even today the majority) this could mean long periods away from base, on tour visiting all parts of the district. For those with an enquiring mind or a scholarly bent, this could mean learning about India in what is still the very best way, living amongst Indians of all classes and witnessing the cycle of the seasons. Some of our most useful knowledge of the ethnography, language, history and religion of India has come from such enthusiasts, 'forced' by virtue of their work to immerse themselves fully in the everyday life of the subcontinent. Historians of modern India have now written substantially about the ICS but the generalisations which are inevitably made to produce ordinary history can sometimes preclude the extraordinary stories of individuals. It is for this reason that I look forward to reading this book – diaries from almost a century ago and recollections of thirty years lived in India. All those interested in that remarkable event which was British India, now rapidly disappearing into history, must be thankful to Janet Richardson for ensuring that her father's knowledge of and enthusiasm for 'his patch' of Bengal is passed on to another generation.

T. Richard Blurton
Dept. of Oriental Antiquities, British Museum
March 2000

PREFACE

My father was always writing something. When we were children he used to write poems for us and it was always he who sent us long letters at boarding school. So, after his death in 1989 it was no surprise to find that he had left us a box of diaries, papers and photographs. At the request of the India Office in 1981, he had written an official account of his service in the ICS in Bengal from 1930-1947, but the papers he wrote for us were not official papers, they were written for his family. I only wish we could have read them during his lifetime and talked to him about them. There is so much more he could have told us and so many interesting photographs he could have identified.

The ICS (Indian Civil Service) has a unique place in the history of the British Empire. An elite group of about a thousand men governed more than 300,000,000 Indians. Known as the 'Heaven Born' – brains, ability, ambition, power – they were responsible for every aspect of their subjects' lives and took their duties very seriously. The ICS and its high ideals are still admired in modern India. The IAS (Indian Administrative Service) carries on the tradition.

Donald MacPherson was the eldest of four children, brought up in Edinburgh at the Royal High School and Edinburgh University, where he read history. After taking the ICS exams he spent a year in London learning Bengali before setting off to India in 1917 at the age of twenty-four. To the best of my knowledge neither he nor his family had ever been abroad before, so it was truly a 'Great Adventure'. The diary of his voyage in 1917 was written for the family back in London Street in Edinburgh. Although I have omitted some parts, I have not altered the style or language, which I felt was typical of the man and the era.

The rest of the recollections were written much later after he had retired. They are a random collection of memories and impressions of his life in India, including a brief period in the Army. It is still amazing to me to read how these young inexperienced men coped so well with the authority and responsibilities thrust upon them by the Empire.

In 1945, after a very successful career in the ICS, Donald returned to

Britain from his final post as Commissioner of Hooghly and Burdwan Division. He was awarded the CIE (Companion of the Indian Empire) in 1946. In retirement he and my mother spent many happy years alternating between their two flats, one in Parkstone, Dorset and the other in his beloved Edinburgh.

Going through all his notes and deciphering his handwriting has been a fascinating and rewarding exercise for me and I hope this book will also be of interest to others, apart from his family and friends and those of us who remember the days of the Raj.

Janet Richardson

Diary of a Voyage to India 1917

November 6th

Today is to see the beginning of the Great Adventure, and the last three days in London have been the overture. All the calls to be paid and the business to be transacted at the last moment have been like the tuning up before the performance begins. Sometimes I was rather annoyed with the futile methods which run this country, but mostly I was surprised that people should be so kind and so hearty in their good wishes. Sometimes I caught myself wishing this voyage was not to be. It would have been so good to remain at home – cold winter, fireless hearth and foodless days notwithstanding. I found that even on the 5th there were things I had forgotten, things I had to buy, and duties I had not fulfilled. Late that night I determined to insure my baggage at all costs.

I shall not easily forget last night – and it was well past candlelight time when I went to bed to sleep only a few hours. I awoke when the night had not yet gone, and could sleep no more. So, by the light of a candle on a chair beside the bed, I wrote the last letters home, the last letters from England. And as I wrote day dawned – it was a grey damp foggy November morning: a drizzle showed on the windows. Surely a most suitable day in which to leave old England. But, as the time went by, the sky cleared and when the *Sardinia* left Tilbury Docks the sun was quite strong.

But the morning was so mixed up as to defy description. Parcels innumerable I had to tie up with paper that was tattered and torn and with the remnants of string. I could hardly decide which thing was to go in which parcel – and when I did at length leave Endsleigh Gardens – the Caledonian Christian Club – I resembled the poor dear Private Secretary who did not like London at all. Four bundles tied by string and a variety of letters and cards deprived me of the power of one hand, while with the other I tried to keep upon my shoulder a bag of golf sticks and other things packed up a quarter of an hour before

1

leaving home. Down to Holborn with Miss Nix – down streets I have so often trod with her or with Saunders. The trees in Russell Square are now about as bare as I imagined they would be in the most luxuriant summer. Bought a book in Mudies, and tried to insure my baggage in Cook's Holborn Office, but the boy and man behind the counter haughtily refused my requests. Nothing daunted, tho' greatly wondering at myself, I tried Cook's Cheapside Office – and found the manager agreeable to what the other had declared impossible.

Chenoy had waited for me at Liverpool Street and, having seen to the baggage, I went to revisit the Institution. Mr Anderson, Mr Cox and Prof. Mill, all of them I saw, and all wished me a good voyage. I am glad that I have met them and known them.

Thereafter things began to move. The train left Liverpool Street in the heart of Western Civilization – and arrived at Tilbury where the platform swarmed with Indian labourers – 'impressed Gujeratis', Chenoy said. Some were little boys – black bright eyes – light brown complexions – dazzling teeth, and light blue overalls. Some had red sashes – others red caps by way of personal adornment. Their chatter was incessant, but when they had taken the parcels on board, they waited as quietly and docilely as horses. There was fuss as one by one each passenger filed thro' a gangway and had his ticket inspected by a Customs Officer and by some Military Gents with red caps. And so I was on board the *Sardinia*.

Not many passengers – and accommodation not what I expected of a P&O. No marble stairways – no luxurious lounges – no spreading palms. But lunch was good and satisfying after all the flying about I had indulged in during the morning. About 1 p.m. we began to move; slowly, slowly we slid away from the quay. Few folk were there to see the ship start, but as she passed through dock after dock, all the men on the small boats ceased their labours and stared at the *Sardinia*. When at last we reached the Thames, the sun was shining brightly over London which was hidden in a golden mist. But the water made a glittering pathway to the Great City. In the Thames till five o'clock when the ship moved quickly, guided by the tiny *Simla*. At 5 p.m. she anchored somewhere off the Kentish coast, the exact situation of which none of us could guess.

Strolling round and round the deck was our only occupation. Reading we tried, but found impossible. My head was funny and my tummy seemed to be agitated like a blancmange. Dinner at 7 p.m. – and a jolly good one too, since food regulations evidently do not apply to P&O

Lines at sea – set me all right. The gentleman at our table told us what to expect on the voyage:
1) Submarine drill
2) Share in keeping watch at all hours of the day and night, and
3) Helping in any emergency.

At least the voyage ought to be exciting. Luckily Shearer, Staig and I share our cabin. I sleep above Shearer, and Staig sleeps below the porthole. After undoing some baggage, and feeling absolutely done out thereby, Staig and I went to bed by 9.30, but Shearer preferred to sit in the smoke room and puff clouds of smoke and watch the mob of officers. Poor soul, some wretch has taken his handbag with his most personal and necessary articles down the hold: and he won't shave until he gets that bag. What are my impressions? I can't say, for I am too sleepy for words.

November 7th
I must have slept soundly – Shearer's belated entrance into the cabin did not disturb me – but at 1 a.m. Staig cried out that we were moving and there was a moon. Sure enough the moonlight haze was beautiful, and we listened to the lapping of the waters in the certainty that we were on our way. But dawn found us where we were at 5 p.m. yesterday afternoon. It seems that everything is not ready and this forenoon is to be spent loading, so while all my friends imagine me tossing on the raging deep and feeling the effects of the rocking of the ship in my innards, I am safely pacing the deck watching the process of loading up. There is a strongish wind blowing – but the cold is not nearly so great as it was at Edinburgh last week.

Shearer's late hours made him a lazy, sleepy dog this morning but, stung by our taunts, he managed to rise after us and seize a basin and be washed and pacing the deck before we had finished shaving. Breakfast was another good solid meal. On board this ship we shall all turn fat as prize porkers. The waiters are all black and at least they do not possess the hauteur and superciliousness of our English waiters. In fact the crew is more or less native to a man – and very funny it was yesterday to see the coal carriers, their work over, sitting in a circle with dirty cloths wrapped over their heads and chattering as hard as tongues can chatter.

The Steward is native too, with a pleasant smile and still more pleasant name. At breakfast conversation turned on a collision last night. I certainly felt the bump, being in the passage on the side of the

3

collision, but until I went on deck and heard the shouting and language I thought the *Sardinia* had weighed anchor. A boat (a tramp steamer) was moving away apologetically into the darkness. Then the stranger at the table turned out to be a Sudan civil servant, and the ways and means of obtaining 'leave' were thrashed out.

The day was spent in walking up and down the promenade deck, now on one side, now on the other according as the wind changed. Sometimes we read, sometimes we wrote up diaries that we are all going to keep. We watched the loading and the various small sailing boats forever hovering around the *Sardinia* and waited for the clock to come round to dinner, luncheon and tea. In the afternoon many a ship passed us outward bound gaily decorated with cubist designs in grey, pink, black and green. Such is the wonderful art of camouflage. The *Sardinia* itself is so bedecked, but its strange appearance is not visible from the promenade deck. The drifters and other small fry plying on the river, crossing the sun's pathway with outspread sails, and the distant haze of chimneys and ships lying at anchor, were a wonderful thing to see. The breeze is freshening and the sea is becoming choppier each moment.

Probably, we shall start at dawn tomorrow, but it may be we shall have to put into Plymouth for three days for repairs as a result of last night's collision. We shall be lucky if we reach Calcutta by Christmas Day. Bored with a weary day of doing nothing, we counted ourselves fortunate in getting a pack of cards which kept us busy to bedtime. But what hands were mine!

November 8th
At early dawn, strictly between six and half past, the *Sardinia* began to put up steam. The engines rumbled away, and the noise was exaggerated in our ears by the rails of the bunk which rang like tuning forks. But it was worthwhile being awake at the moment the big sailing began. At first it was the changed feel of the cabin, then the passing of the landmarks that proved we were launched on the road to Bombay. Thereafter we dozed till breakfast time in happy contentment. After breakfast the problem of the day and how the hours were to be spent stared us straight in the face. The sea had lost its novelty, England was little more than a strip on the horizon, and none of us knew our exact location. Promenading the deck has now only one object – exercise; and no pleasure can be taken in it, especially as the wind has risen and a wet driving mist has made the Channel and sky one uniform grey. In

the forenoon our eyes were cheered by the sight of many vessels plying to and fro. Some of these must have been our Convoy. It was reassuring to feel that one was in the heart of such a throng of shipping.

About lunchtime we passed Dover. We were hugging coast and the white cliffs were clearly visible, and the stations perched above them by Dover Harbour and Castle. The view was good, and in the neighbourhood were numberless destroyers cutting the waves. On the Southern horizon rising about a quarter of an inch above it were the cliffs of Calais, like ours of Dover. According to the time-honoured precedent, the glimpse of the White Cliffs should have filled me with poignant emotion. But I felt nothing at all. Perhaps because I come from Scotland and the Tweed for me takes the place of the famous cliffs. What chiefly annoyed me was the wind which, blowing hard from the West, blew my new cap into the sea. It must have cost me about 6*d*. every time I wore that cap. The cap had blown off before – but it had scudded along the deck and I had been able fairly easily to recapture it. But on this second occasion the sea received it. Bridge filled the afternoon – not very exciting certainly – yet better than thinking on when the roll will make one seasick.

The doctor says we are in for a bad night of it. Perhaps we shall sleep in our 'warmest clothing' as the notice puts it. After lunch we were all told to carry our lifebelts about with us wherever we went. They are to be beside us at meals, and beside us at bedtime. They are most uncomfortable things tying round one's neck. The tapes of mine barely meet twice round my waist. Let's hope we won't need them. As yet there has been no 'boat drill' – but all day the crew has been getting the boats (8 of them) down on to a level with the deck and, once that is all in order, we ought to have that to relieve the monotony of the days. There is no equivalent of them except a wet Sunday in dingy country lodgings. Tomorrow we are expecting to be at Plymouth, and then I may have time to write a letter home.

One of the officers on board plays the violin really well – a little music now and again will help to relieve matters, for there is a limit to one's reading capacities. I don't know what I am writing – my head is wagging from side to side with a giddy sort of feeling. Not sickness I hope – but the roll is developing and I now know what a courageous man Columbus was to dare the wild unknown Atlantic in a rickety second hand wooden tub. All honour to him! There is a Naval Officer on board who some weeks ago was blown up at sea – and here he is going off to West Africa. He has been recommended for some distinction, but such incidents are all in the day's work so he has to go without. Some folks have rotten luck.

A funny queerness has been developing in my head all day – and by dinner I was fairly miserable. When at last I had eaten thro' all the six courses I was jolly thankful that it had passed without serious mishap. After a blow on a pitch deck, where the waves seemed to be washing, we three adjourned to our bunks to relieve the queerness. Each took a book and within three minutes was fast asleep.

November 9th

Wakened to find I had slept with my glasses. After the queerness of last night I felt quite refreshed by the night's rest. The morning was beautifully clear, and thro' the porthole we saw the Devon fishing fleet returning across the track of the early morning sun. Their sails were reddish and contrasted with the deeper blue of the sea, and with the green of the Devon coasts. We were hugging the land, and had a magnificent view of these famous rocky shores. At first it was hard to locate ourselves – and bill after bill, bay after bay was passed until we came to Plymouth Sound. Early in the day a British Monster Submarine was sighted, some two miles off, and far too distant to give us an idea of anything except its size; and soon afterwards the sound of repeated firing was heard. It was only an innocent looking old wooden sailing ship mounted with a gun, calling on a mystery ship away on the horizon to stop until it had submitted to an inspection by one of our watchdogs. Far to the South, rising like a needle, we saw the famous Eddystone Lighthouse. And so, in calm weather with a fair sky, a steady wind and blue sea, we sailed up Plymouth Sound, and anchored off Plymouth. The country was greener than any I had left, and the famous Drake's Island from the deck seemed to have something sub-tropical – something romantic about it. We are too far out to distinguish the various interesting places of the town, which appears very scattered. Sufficient we have seen the Hoe – and the first news we heard was that we are to sleep for many nights near Plymouth Hoe.

It is strange to think of the world wagging along, and not to hear a sough of all its worries. The Pilot brought strange tidings.
1) Revolution in Russia – which rumour had enlarged and made picturesque.
2) That Marseilles is a closed port owing to the Italian affair, and that we shall have to wait for the overland passengers here. Poor Desai and De Kretzer!

3) That our Convoy left yesterday.

Some of the passengers would go ashore, and about three got into a Customs boat which came alongside. One is a Naval Officer called Jellicoe weighing 22 stone and having girth measurement of yards! It was truly wonderful to see him descend the rickety rope ladder. He was purple when he reached the bottom rung.

In the afternoon many queer new boats passed out and in – destroyers, patrol boats and others built like submarines. Being at anchor and at peace our feelings were relieved and we could pass the evening at cards and reading quite enjoyably.

A letter came for me today – strange to have one so far away and yet so near from England. The voyage may not be so boring after all.

November 10th

The ship is riding at anchor in Plymouth Sound – and the absence of rolling made rising into the fresh morning most enjoyable. Before breakfast a boy came alongside with papers, the first we had seen for three days, and much had happened in the interval. It was pleasant idling away time, with the hills to the North. The weather was fine, and the sea peaceful. Music, cards and watching the lascars haul up from the hold the baggage of those who joined in the afternoon. They were more careful than the railway porters, and it was wonderful in what good condition the baggage was. From lunch onward there was the excitement of waiting for those that were arriving. There was to be a rearrangement of berths so great was the crush and, moreover, those who had gone ashore were to return with the tender. It was later than anyone bargained for. After we had sunk into apathy owing to repeated false alarms of its arrival, it drew alongside about 6.00, when dusk had already settled down. By the light of a lantern the forms of last night's roysterers could be picked out, and Jellicoe was received with a mighty cheer as he stepped on board. Dé, Desai and De Kretzer were there, much wearied by such hasty preparation, having only been warned of the change of route on Thursday morning. Dé had had to arrange his passports in one day. But here they were. Dinner was a slower affair than it had been previously – but on that account probably better for my digestion. The promenade deck was lit till a late hour, and littered with bundles and packages of all sizes, which frenzied passengers tried to identify. The presence of Dé, Desai and De Kretzer induced us three to keep late hours.

7

November 11th

A Sunday! My first at sea, but were it not for the Calendar, I would not have known. However, although everything seemed to go as usual, a sacrifice was made to conventions when it was decided to have no rag times! The addition to the passengers makes a vast difference. The Steward cannot give us his undivided attention, and did not waken us. He did not come near us until I had jumped out of my bunk. Outside the bathroom there was a crowd waiting for the use of the bath – and many went away unwashed rather than stand in a queue. This is the only restriction. Moreover from an early hour, some early birds had paced the deck above our heads, and their regular tread had disturbed our slumbers.

After breakfast boat drill was down on the programme of the day – at 10 o'clock. But it was not exciting. Every passenger assembled on the Hurricane Deck over against his boat with his life jacket tied on. That was all. The Stewards showed how they should be tied for the greatest security. Then after a little trifling would-be amusing conversation followed by dismissal we lazed thro' the forenoon, speculating the hour of starting – and spreading wild rumours of intended routes.

Meantime many warships and JBDs began to leave Plymouth and, towards the end of lunch, the porthole disclosed the land moving away. Slowly we left the South. Above us hovered an aeroplane, before us was a cruiser and, on either side, destroyers. We kept well to the Western coastline – and passed Eddystone rising from a foundation of waters. For long the shores of Devon and Cornwall remained in sight, but towards dusk they vanished. Still the cruiser and destroyers guard us, and reassure us with every sight we have of them.

Cards filled up the evening. What else was there to do? And we were far from being the only breakers of the Sabbath. Just before bedding – when it was impossible to make out objects on deck – I saw the lights of the cruiser and destroyers, and they were flashing messages to each other. Staig and Shearer are rather scornful of De Kretzer and his Great Life-saving Waistcoat and re-tell with gusto how he paled at the sound of one steam whistle (five blasts being danger signal), but they sleep in their warmest clothing in case of emergencies!

November 12th

All this day we sailed to the South West, for the sun was ever on the right. Beside us, heartening us, was the Convoy. Now it sped ahead of us, now it zig-zagged to the right of us. Sometimes it trailed behind us. Seagulls innumerable followed in our wake, being persuaded at Plymouth that the garbage of Sardinia would be a satisfactory source of food. Ever and anon we passed through mist and fog and rain and, as mist obscured the distance, our Escort came near us. In early morning the sea was, in Homeric phrase, wine-coloured, but beneath brighter skies its colour became a deeper richer blue, and at night the foam on the waves gleamed a ghostly white in the darkness.

November 13th
I have been a week on board ship and I am becoming used to the queer cramped and withal aimless life. Last Tuesday I was hurrying down Holborn – today I see nothing but the waste of waters. Cards and walking round the deck (promenade fashion) is all there is to occupy our minds. Some folk seem to find it bearable, others look bored with everything and principally with themselves, and justly too, for theirs is the fault of being bored. Staig tried to do a little work this morning – but desisted after a very short struggle with virtuous intentions and, before I had time to follow his example, I was hauled off to accompany on the piano for about an hour or so. The piano is in a most awkward position. It stands at the head of the stairs leading to the saloon – and at either side of the landing is a door which opens on to the deck. If one is close all is well but, sure as fate, no sooner have I come to the most ticklish part of an accompaniment than a Goan steward, brush and shovel in hand, opens the closed door. There is a gust of wind, a frantic effort to catch the music from falling from the broken stand – and then a scramble to retrieve it as it tosses on the floor. Meantime the violin goes on singing its passionate songs. It is hard thereafter to find the place, and take up the accompaniment. And again we must not play or sing between the hours of two and four, for then the Captain sleeps. An Edinburgh man yesterday asked me to give some piano support to his strong bass voice, and he was putting the full force of a well developed and strong organ into a Mozartian thing. Quick came the steward bounding up the steps three at a time. 'You mustn't, you mustn't. I am sorry but the Captain sleeps!' And he lifted the music from the piano and the poor man was left high and dry and speechless on his topmost note. Later in the evening playing is impossible owing to the lighting restrictions.

I don't know where we are – but we must be about 15 degrees West. The clocks have not been put back to time corresponding with the latitude, and so we noticed that the sun seemed to rise and set very late. Everybody was not on deck for the rising, but most of the passengers enjoyed the setting and Venus shining clear and bright above the still glowing Western horizon. The ship seems to be heading due South – but the Escort has departed. Two days journey from Plymouth is what its duties were: and we shall probably be met by an Escort from Gibraltar. Another ship is with us – it is small but fast, and crosses from one to the other side of us for some reason I know not of.

The aloofness and strangeness of the passengers is wearing off – cliques and groups are being formed. We six from the ICS form a class apart. Already games have made their appearance in a tentative way, such as rope quoits and skipping. Two ladies were among the crowd that arrived at Plymouth: and their attentions are much in demand. They need never have a leisure moment – and certainly ought to enjoy themselves! But they are rather plain!

The brightness of the white foam I noticed last night is due to phosphorescence in the water, which makes the foam glisten as if lit by electricity. There were sparks of light showing in the water, where fishes swam near the surface and the boat seemed to make a light as it cut the waves. Afar the crests of the waves seemed alive with water spirits ever dancing upon them. It was wonderful, especially when one had come from the smoke-laden atmosphere of the saloon, where everybody had gathered for the sole recreation of the night – cards. Cards, I must say, always leave me tired and ready for bed. I tried to read – but managed two lines and the book had to be taken from my hand.

November 14th
Daily the sky is becoming clearer. Daily the water is becoming deeper and deeper blue. There is a warmth in the air, and the passengers are beginning to sport golfing jackets and white shoes. At times something of a hilarity prevails but the afternoon is principally devoted to sleep. Dé, Staig and De Kretzer are the greatest devotees – while Desai and I gallantly promenade the deck in order to acquire an appetite for afternoon tea. After tea two great balls were produced and some strenuous men got themselves into form by pitching these weighty objects from one to the other.

In the morning great trouble is created by there being only one bathroom for some fifty men. About 7.30 there is a rush and a queue always forms – and Shearer had to wait some 15 minutes today to have his splash. Otherwise there is nothing to record. We had music in the forenoon and the officer who plays the violin had a fairly long discussion with me on art and other topics. He is awfully decent. A strange thing happened. A fat man with protruding eyes came up and spoke to me. It turns out he is a brother of a man Shearer was instructed to be sure and call upon. He hails from Broughty Ferry.

November 15th

Still the sea is around us on all sides; the earth is bounded by a circular horizon some five miles off. We have been speculating as to where we are – but without result. The Doctor says we shall probably be at Gib by Saturday. Let us hope so. I began rummaging in my box today for lighter things – I may not be out of the swim too long: and the others turned in to see. During the process a good deal of the shortbread made a much appreciated translation to another sphere. Surely we are near the latitude of Gib. The sun is high in the heavens and the atmosphere fine and clear. This evening when the sun dipped below the horizon darkness followed in a few seconds, as is the way in tropical and sub-tropical parts. I was writing on deck and the Doctor called me to attention for wasting my eyes when the light had gone.

When we have nothing else to do we watch some ponies which are being sent to Bombay – but today diversion was caused by a pet monkey in the bow. After it had jumped and twisted about in all sorts of antics it was taken in hand by one of the officers who, accompanied by two others, one with a banjo, made the round of the ship collecting coppers or silver – a pleasant interlude in the afternoon. This was not the only collecting done this day. In the morning a sweepstake was arranged. Everyone took tickets and the names were put into a hat, from which they were drawn with numbers attached. The numbers were to represent the distance travelled in the last 24 hours. The lucky passengers were from the 2nd class – the distance travelled being given approximately by the Captain as 214 miles. Thus we have been travelling much slower than any of us expected.

Just after dinner Desai and I went on deck for a stroll and a digestive rest. The stars were brilliant and Venus made a pathway of light upon the sea. But in a few minutes the brightness was dimmed and, before we turned in, she had faded and sunk below the horizon. The Plough was dipping its handle in the waters of the North, and somewhere in the East a star was rising into a brilliance equal to that of Venus which had set in the West. When, after an hour's indulgence at cards, I went

11

on deck once again with Staig, the change in the position of the stars in relation to the horizon was most obvious. I knew this happened but never before had I witnessed it with my own eyes. Tobacco is duty-free – wherefore Shearer has and smokes nothing less than cigars now. He thinks it gives him a plutocratic appearance – Ho ho!

November 16th

All agog with thoughts that Gib will be reached tomorrow. In the forenoon another sweepstake was arranged, but how it is to be financed I know not. I was persuaded to buy one ticket – and was nowhere in the running. Certain numbers were drawn, and these were auctioned by Jellicoe looking very fat and jolly. But after the first enthusiasm, bidding grew less furious. A huge Convoy of some seven Merchant ships was sighted on the horizon, going either westward or to the Northwest. And in a short time another vessel was sighted in the distance – and again another. Even with field glasses their outlines were faint and dim. Just before lunch a notice was posted up stating there would be a despatch at 12 midnight. Oh! what a busy afternoon ensued – everybody was busy writing at once. The paper supply ran out very often. Even De Kretzer, who usually spends his afternoons in bed, sat on deck with a writing pad before him. Tea finished, land came in sight. At first it was hard to say whether the misty outline of the hills was not cloud, but gradually it lengthened and strengthened. Soon we could distinguish the African from the Spanish mountains, and some believed they saw the dark outline of the rock of Gib. Ships were no longer the rare sight they had been of late. The night came on earlier, since all day we had been travelling eastward and the difference in longitude made itself perceptible. It was at this time that I had agreed to play a final set of accompaniments to the RWF Officer's violin solos. Judge of our dismay when we found the roof lights of the saloon with drawn blinds. His E string had broken and, by the time he had a new one fixed in, twilight had fallen. The playing was done under difficulties; and before we had finished the stewards had started shutting up. The 'Chant sans Paroles' was a scramble: halfway thro' the music pages fluttered downwards, and then the darkness was so thick that the last notes were played by memory. When we came on deck again still more land was seen, and lights picked out the main points.

About 8.00 the glimmer of Tangiers was visible but for long doubt hung over its identity. I had promised to play bridge but, watching the approach to the land with Desai, I was loath to go downstairs. Before dinner I had a long conversation with the Officer about the beautiful sunset of deep orange, graduating into the deep blue. In this heavy colour sailed the crescent moon of palest silver, and beyond it Venus herself. Two weeks ago I should have said these tints were not of Nature – but now I know them, and love them. We discussed photography, especially that of the setting sun. Altho' I had a cold in the head, and the breeze blowing round the land was chilly, I could not resist the joy of waiting until the ship had come to anchor in Gibraltar Bay. About 10.00 I went on deck and the doctor was there to help us with the names of the places we passed. Tangiers slipped by at ten, and on the Spanish side a lighthouse (not an important one, but sending three short flashes after a considerable interval) lit the deck. We must have been sailing about two miles from the coast.

Soon we came to Gib – and from then onwards the deck was crowded with those who watched the safe arrival of the *Sardinia*. To the left lay Algeciras – a small streak of lights. Gib itself lay to the right and we could trace the town by the small lights showing. Occasionally there would be a signal flashed from the rock, and guarding the harbour were three powerful searchlights. Twice they were turned on us and night became as day. Truly it was a magnificent sight, the sleeping town guarded by an ever wakeful watch, and the incoming ship.

About 12.00 the anchor held – and there our participation in the proceedings ended, for we were so tired that bed was an absolute necessity. I believe that the final anchorage of the ship was not fixed till about 1.00, but by that time we were asleep. Even a fight among the lascars could not disturb us. Will we see Gib more closely? I hope so! It is sure to be interesting – even if only a change from the eternal sea and ship.

November 17th

Saturday. Despite our unusual hours I was early awake. De Kretzer called us on the back of six and, lazy dog! went back to bed again pursued by maledictious words not deeds! Last night was the first on which he had a proper rest. He found no submarines.

It was glorious to see Gib in the early morning with the sun just rising behind the rock, and glinting white on the houses of Algeciras across the bay. In our discussions as to which way we entered last night we became quite heated, and when Spanish dock labourers came aboard to help with the unloading and, by gesticulations and swearing, tried to make themselves understood to the lascars, they swore back in

Hindustani all together. The few white men supervising grew red in the face and swore in English, so there was sufficient activity to distract our attention.

Some of the passengers were preparing to land, and the others watched them with longing eyes. About ten to ten a notice posted up on the Companion announced that a launch would leave at 10.00 for Gib – and would return at 12.30 and 4.30. What a hurry! I got out my new golf jacket and sported it in spite of my cold. It was a chance not to be missed – and we all went on shore. Crossing to Gib there was probability of a thunderstorm and I was regretting my choice of coats – unnecessarily as it turned out. For the day was glorious and I enjoyed myself beyond my wildest dreams.

After the necessary preliminaries as to examination of passports had been gone through, we issued from the water port into an open market, where fruit and meat (such meat!) was being sold. Beneath the arch of the waterport sat an old wrinkled hag selling drinks. 'Twas the first sign of the new country. In the market swaggered a swarthy Moor, tall and strong as Othello, with bright yellow cloak and slippered feet. Thence into the main street, swarming with folks out marketing. Already at 11.00 they were returning home laden with their purchases – and were not content with walking but used the quaint light Gib car. It seats four – and driver – and except for the curtains draped at each side, is open. Later in the day we saw a bridal party spin along the street in these cars, the bridesmaids much more handsome than the bride. Perhaps the black mantillas set off their beauty more than the silvery veil and orange blossom of the bride. People seemed to wander about aimlessly hailing one another, the shopkeepers standing at their doors. Our entrance evidently bestirred them, since I heard one say to another that a P&O must have arrived during the night time.

The main street is mean and narrow; the shops are all small. The junior Army & Navy Stores appeared no larger than a second rate ironmonger's in a provincial town, while there were a great number of Oriental bazaars kept by Indians displaying all manner of laces, ivories (principally imitation) and gaily worked Japanese silk things. De Kretzer knew someone in Gib and went off to find him, but he kept us waiting such an age that we went off without him. Lucky that we did so. He never returned to explain what had happened to him. No guidebooks were procurable – so we decided to follow the main street. Now it narrowed, now it widened into a broad pathway lined with trees. On both sides small streets opened off – those to the left heading to the Spanish Quarters, and those to the right to the Docks.

Shearer and Dé were not very enterprising, and soon Dé returned for the early boat; but Staig, Desai and I had come out to see, and we took the higher road, which climbed the rock and led eventually to Europa Point. According to a policeman, every part of the road was open, an untruth we only discovered when we met a sentry at a barrack gate. He was evidently pleased to meet people from England, and in the night time had noted the arrival of the *Sardinia.*

The stone of the Rock seemed to be some hard limestone much contorted, and with a feel akin to that of marble. Halfway along this road Desai exclaimed, 'Look at the submarine,' and close into the coast we saw the back of it like a whale's back, the foam it made cutting the water. Then it submerged. The view across the bay to Algeciras and the hills beyond was magnificent. Beyond the mainland stands another hill smaller than Gib and green to the summit whereon is a little excrescence. This is the Queen of Spain's chair and here she will sit until Gib becomes Spanish once more! Rocky as the slopes of Gib are, there was a considerable amount of vegetation. Cacti were the most numerous, but a sort of convolvulus and small roses were also to be seen. The houses were all square with flat ochre painted sides, and red glazed tile roofs. According to Desai this is a remnant of Moorish architecture, for similar tiles are used in the Moslem part of India. Down below, clustering round the Europa Point side of the Bay – Bay Rosia – it was wonderful to look down on the red tiled houses, each with its little enclosed garden.

This part of the town is chiefly military – we passed barracks, army offices, ASC Stores and dept. stores as we went downwards. Such a steep hill it was, and so rough! In this part of the town there was nothing especially interesting, except the enormous number of barber's shops. Every other shop is a Tommy's Barber. Nevertheless it was evident that here Spain and her lazy old ways was trying to suit herself to English customs – the customs of the Barrack town. Every now and then a cluster of old houses with birds outside and sprawling girls of about thirteen struck a truly Spanish note. Into the main street again and, by good luck, we lit upon a fine place for lunch. The tables proclaimed the pleasures of Batger's Xmas Crackers, by means of a gaily coloured picture of a harlequin. But the meat pies and the cakes were splendiferous, and the chocolate a treat, even without any of the sugar added. We returned here for tea, and my appetite succumbed only after I had downed six of these cakes.

During lunch a flock of turkeys, sleek and glossy, was driven along the main street without any casualties from the racing cars. Shearer had wanted to see me smoke a cigar – had been beastly superior upon the subject. Wherefore, since tobacco was cheap, I smoked a huge Havana – and it was jolly good too and very mild. Staig and Shearer wished to sample Spanish wines and did so in the afternoon, but Desai and I were more adventurous. We saw a submarine at close quarters in the docks (E 59 I think it was); toured round Commercial Square where a Paddy's Market was being held; passed the English Cathedral (a modern building in the Moorish fashion) and the Governor's Quarters. Then we decided to climb the rock and see the Spanish Town.

Hardly had we turned from the main street than the character of the buildings and the atmosphere of the place changed. The streets were narrower – and dirtier: the people had less to do and hung idly about. Streets of steps ascended the rock, and they were bounded on both sides by high ochre-coloured houses. And as we went higher the Spanish element became more and more in evidence. Water was only to be had at the public fountains and round these congregated chattering crowds. Far past the buildings we went until we came to one of the inevitable Trespasser Boards. But the view of the deep blue bay, of the shipping and of Spain beyond was magnificent. The *Sardinia* was lying near to the harbour, amongst the ships in the outer bay. This was the first time that its passengers had seen its gaily painted sides. It was the only camouflaged boat in the bay.

I gathered some dry prickly thistle before retracing my steps and re-entering the maze of alleys and ramps, as these streets of steps are called. Usually they are named after someone famous in Gibraltar's history. There we saw Azenzo's Ramp, Crutchett's Ramp (there was also a Crutchett's Bastion), and Rodger's Ramp!

Here the women sat at their latticed windows, gazing on the passers-by, and the over-laden donkeys with bulging panniers carried the produce of the Spanish orchards to the people's houses. Cruelty to animals must be one of the traits of the local character, since at every other corner was an SPCA sign. At one place a little boy carried an immense terracotta water jar – broken doubtless but of immemorial shape: at another, two women with gay dresses and flowers in their hair squatted round an open basket and cracked nuts monkey fashion. Most of the women are handsome and their black mantillas set off their dark complexions and fine carriage, which is probably inherited from ancestresses who carried everything on their heads. Even today I saw some old country wives carrying large flat baskets of fruit upon their heads. Fruit was in every corner and, where there was no fruit seller, a little boy cooked chestnuts. Some, dusty and ready, were spread before him; others, red and uncooked, were heaped up to supply his little stove. It was a funny stove in which coke was used. Like a drainpipe it stood with a queer shaped pot on top and the boy fanned the coke to a glow with a round fan.

Wandering through these curious streets we came upon a few old houses dating back to Moorish times. Desai pointed out to me the narrow bricks which are used in the old buildings of Mohammedan India. They are glazed, rich red and of irregular shapes. Above them could be traced modern additions of plaster and of brick. But new or old, all were picturesque. With the passing of years the style of architecture cannot have changed much. One particularly fine doorway must have been ancient. It was of wood, and above the door was carved wood of a very simple geometrical pattern. The finish, however, was exquisite. Even the modern doorways had pretty fanlights or grilles of bent iron. Most of these were semi-circular. Many a half-closed doorway we peered into, and caught glimpses of tiled walls, and of tiny flower-covered courtyards. Wonderful places of lights and shadows. The most interesting buildings were Azenzo's Palace, the Church and the Old Moorish Fort. I had never heard of Azenzo – nor did I see more of his Palace than the Gateway and the garden beyond. It was a hanging garden and reached by a long flight of steps. The road led to the right of it under a curious impressive old archway where the round was caught halfway by the advancing wall while, further in, a complete arch was formed. Above was a garden, and purple flowers trailed over the parapet, which ended in a sort of square tower. Among the cluster of buildings in the vicinity we saw a remarkably fine grille with a background of foliage. In the foreground a child was having its after-dinner siesta.

The Church at one period must have been fine. Some especially beautiful carving remained on a round window: a square smug tower with four pinnacles had been stuck on at one side and a tasteful frontage made of some cement stuff added. The Moorish Fort was made of brick and its walls were thick and, although covered with plants, were stout in their decay. I know nothing of the history of the place – it must have been exciting since Gib has always been strategically important; but ignorance of the past could not diminish the impressiveness which the rugged strength of the place called forth.

17

And when we came to the fort, we had travelled over most of the places which can be visited without a pass. Notices – 'Persons are not permitted beyond this spot' – are to be met with everywhere. So we travelled downwards to the Main Street, and collected strange inscriptions. Here are two:

'Ally Shoper and Allies' Hairdresser – Barber.'

Also,

'Orient Bazaar – S. Premchand Bros. Very cheap Jack.'

I am sorry I have not been able to give a better description of this pleasant place – its colours, its smells, its ramps. There were no postcards to be had of it, and those I sent off were commonplace views of the Rock. Down in the Main Street the sun seemed to have hidden behind clouds. The glamour seemed to have gone from the afternoon. We had tea and it was time to hurry for the boat which left for the *Sardinia* at 4.30. But before going on the quay I could not resist going through the Market and I found what I had been looking for – green figs at 3*d*. a pound. And here I rid myself of the curious collection of coppers – Spanish and French – that I had picked up during the day. On the quay we all assembled and by 4.30 were sailing back to the *Sardinia*.

Unfortunately some of the 2nd class passengers had made themselves beasts with drink, and the wonder was that they arrived without being in the water. In the evening Gib lit up was like a fairy city: for near the foot of the Rock were two searchlights which illuminated some old hulks in the bay and which gave a peculiar charm to the view of the town. Unfortunately I had developed a cold and the evening at cards was not as pleasant as it might have been. Or was it the Spanish cakes I had for tea aided by sundry oranges, figs and one Havana?

November 18th

Second Sunday on board – and it was vastly different from the first. The exertions of yesterday had proved too much for most people so, when the tender arrived this morning, only a select few went to Gib. I stayed on board partly because of my cold, partly because I had made up my mind to go tomorrow if that were possible. So I sunned myself, looked at Gib from many points of view, watched the unloading of the ship (sackloads of sugar and flour for the Garrison) and the arrival of the supplies to support us on to Valetta; and wrote up the diary.

And now I find I have not described the situation of the bay. It is deep and round – Gib is at the Eastern side, and Europa Point extends a little more to the South than the Western extremity. The country all around is hilly except for a short strip of land to the North of the rock, which is as flat as the proverbial pancake.

During the day we took on the survivors of the crew of a submarined liner! What a curious assortment of types and races they were, as they bore their bedding and baggage on board. In the afternoon a pale young curate approached me and asked if I played the piano, since he intended to have Divine Service at 8.15 p.m. I assented. Then he enquired if I had ever played hymns! – from sight he hastened to explain. So everything was fixed up and at 8.10 I crossed to the Second Saloon and found the Curate and other missionaries busy over hymn books. The Service was the familiar and beautiful General Confession and Evening Prayer of the Anglican Church; and the hymns we sung were 'The Day Thou gavest Lord is ended', 'For those in Peril on the Sea', 'Jesu Lover of my Soul' and another, the name of which I forget. During his address, which was short and to the point if not very original and illuminating, he had an inspiration: namely that if anyone wanted a favourite hymn sung he had only to speak out. Two of them were sung: one being 'Suns of my Soul' to a most execrable monotonous tune, which a YMCA man thought exquisite – and differed from everybody else in so doing. It was a strange gathering in the low-roofed bare room, but it was really a great occasion: and I recalled as I played how often and in what different times and places I had sung and accompanied these hymns.

My cold is no better. I got a friend to buy eucalyptus from shore and had to ask the stewards for lumps of sugar. Before going to bed I had a glass of hot toddy. I had great difficulty in explaining the nature of this to our steward who knows little English. However, I managed to make him understand. He is greatly distressed none of us take tea in bed before rising – and when he suggested fruit and I snapped at that suggestion, a whole load of worry seemed to roll away from him, and his face brightened with wreathed smiles.

November 19th
Still at Gib – but the tender took no passengers on shore today; wherefore we all lazed and complained of boredom – a thing unheard of until we had a good exciting time on Saturday. Everyone agog with a notice asking for volunteers for a submarine lookout – not to warn about a submarine in the offing, but that a submarine be sent to Davy Jones. Everyone was pencilling down their names so, without reading

the notice through, I did so too. But at breakfast I was told there was an eyesight clause. Thereupon I scratched out my name and asked the doctor if I had done right, and he agreed.

It seems the winter rains of the Mediterranean are three weeks late already, so unless there is to be a terrible time next year, the rains are expected any day. This led to a discussion of the dessication of the globe. Perhaps the boat will start in the night, at any rate when the lists of the submarine watches were put up Shearer and De Kretzer were on the 1st Watch which, if the boat starts at night, will begin at 6.00. Staig and I are wondering how Shearer will rise to the occasion next morning. We must sleep lightly and with one eye open.

According to some accounts, we have passed through the worst zone of U-boat activity when we were nearing Gib on Friday, and that was the day of days on our southward voyage on which our thoughts of submarines was least. Let us hope this is true.

Gib looked wonderful tonight – with its rows of lights seen through the silvery haze of the searchlights which, in their turn, lit up some old hulks in dazzling white. There was a pearly grey mist over the bay, and it seemed that the black forms of the boats anchored behind us rode on the night air. I wish Mother were here for a few days with her pencil, her watercolours and her sketchbook!

November 20th
Shearer roused himself at 5.20 all right. I saw him wash himself thro' half-closed eyelids, and remember nothing more until the fruit was brought. And Shearer was in bed. The ship did not start until 8 o'clock, and Shearer's watch did not begin until 9.20. The Escort proved to be a British JBDavid and right glad we all were, having a feeling that the escort duty might be undertaken by Americans or Japs. We had seen both in Gib – especially the American sailors who swarmed all over the place, wearing little white caps like those cooks wear.

Our progress at first was slow, as we steamed out of the bay and round Europa Point – very much treated with concrete – into the Mediterranean. There was our best opportunity of viewing Gibraltar as a whole and getting it placed in relation to Spain and the Mediterranean. From a distance it looks rather like a flattened rocky Arthur's Seat – and it remains visible long after all the neighbouring country has died out of sight.

We kept hugging the Spanish coast for safety. The coast looked only a mile off, but in this clear atmosphere appearances are deceptive.

Perhaps we were cruising in Spain's territorial waters; perhaps we were without the three mile limit. Opinions differed but, at any rate, we had a magnificent panorama of the Spanish hills which run down to the sea. They rose from its very edge and towered over the narrow strip of coastal plain, on which were a few towns. The mountains were brown and dry, with channels where water courses had been. The rains have not yet come. They are overdue but, once they appear, those channels will fill up and the brown hillsides will be verdant. Perched on barren slopes were many white houses – homesteads depending on the vineyards. With the sun right overhead the terracing of these was invisible, but with the lengthening shadows the rows of plants were thrown into relief. It was only with the onset of twilight that the distance of the hills could be appreciated, for then the valleys filled with purple hues, while the nearer coast was golden with the rays of the setting sun.

Twice in the course of the afternoon a discussion as to whether the distant peaks were slightly covered with snow, and were therefore the off shoots of the Sierra Nevada, was interrupted by the sight of smoke rising from one of the coastal heights. These, according to the doctor, were smoke signals for submarines – but mayhap he indulges in pulling the legs of landlubbers. The evening set in early – on the back of five, for we have been travelling eastward – and it was magnificent. We expected to leave Spain behind in the darkness, but about 10.30 it could still be made out looming a few miles to the northward.

November 21st
This week, if nothing else happens, we shall appear on the list of ships unsuccessfully attacked. The morning was glorious – and there were two sides at breakfast holding contrary opinions as to whether what we saw on the Northern horizon was a belt of cloud or the snowy peaks of Spain. Question was never settled. I proved my moral courage by refusing to partake in the chances of a sweepstake in the morning and helped Dé to unpack and fix up his gramophone. With the amount of straw in the boxes it was easy for little parts to be lost. Then after lunch we had a small concert in his cabin, the tunes ranging from violin solos as played by the Great Masters to the latest ragtimes. For the convenience of the neighbours we stopped it at 2.30 – and I had just gone on deck, leaving my life-saving jacket with companions, when I noticed something was up.

All the lascars were gathered on the poop in a very excited state –

21

some had bundles, all had their cork jackets on. There was a great noise of chattering: some pointed to sea – then began to run to the deck. Suddenly the steam whistle blew twice: I was waiting for the other three blasts, when there was the noise of a gunshot. Still I could not believe anything serious was up, but to make sure went for my lifejacket and put it on somehow and then made for boat No. 4. Everybody was gathering there – everybody was looking either for warm things or their lifejackets. There was no confusion: only a great expectancy. Staig came down from the watch tying the strings round his waist, and Shearer followed him closely. Then as we had time, it seemed, to look around Staig and I retrieved our waterproofs. Still nothing happened and on our side most of the passengers were interested in a man who was busy getting into a suit like a diver's. It was a most weird creation – fitted with all sorts of pads, and inflated belts and with things to keep one's spirits up when in the water. Had there been very sudden necessity for taking to the boats he would have been left half in and half out of his life-saving clothes.

Dé, Desai and Kretzer had soon sped up from their cabin and were ready when their Steward was absent and could nowhere be found. Far on the horizon we could see our Escort cruising about; black, thick smoke came from its funnels leaving a long track. This may have been a smoke cloud but it seemed to me to lend prominence to the destroyer's position. In a short time it returned with a red and white flag, and the *Sardinia* replied with another red and white flag. Danger was past: we were safe for the time being. A morse message was signalled from the destroyer which, according to later rumours, said that the two depth charges which the JBD had dropped in the vicinity from where the U-boat had fired the torpedo ought to have been effective, and that it was confidently hoped that this pest had been removed from the seas for ever.

And then came the stories. Staig had been on watch but at the side opposite to that on which the submarine was sighted and had had a difficult time in getting to his boat as he had to breast a crowd of lascars swarming on to the upper deck. Some were very excited, having had former experience of being torpedoed, and the threat of shooting had to be applied. Some dropped their bundles into the boats – to be sure of saving something; some dropped into the boats before any signal was given. Shearer had been without his life-saving jacket when the steam whistle blew and, in going to the cabin, heard a sort of meeting amongst the stokehold crew. It seems the submarine – or perhaps there were two – had been seen for about half an hour. The conning tower of one had been sighted on the horizon just against the sun, then it had disappeared. Most of the passengers were ignorant of what was taking place until the steam whistle went off. It found not a few undressed and in the realms of Morpheus, and the signal was not given until the torpedo was fired. The ship had immediately turned in its course and thus saved itself from disaster, which was pretty close. When the white line of the torpedo was seen it was fifty yards, not more, from the stern of the ship and, after allowing for the rate at which the *Sardinia* and the torpedo were travelling at the time it passed, it could not have been more than ten yards away from the propeller. So narrow was our escape – yet everything on board went with mechanical precision, and an air raid was many times more terrible. We are all careful of our life-saving jackets now.

In the evening a moon arose and, although it had a watery halo, it shone brightly and illuminated the sea. Alas! we have no greater desire than any harassed Londoner for nights of moonlit loveliness. The fact that there had been no subsequent attack at night was cheering. Either the U-boat had been done for or was thoroughly scared!

November 22nd
Today fulfilled the promise of last night's stormy moon: but what we encountered was only the outskirts of a violent tempest in the Gulf of Lions. Glad we were that we were travelling eastward, since we had not to breast the waves. The roll in itself was bad enough; and often our Escort hurrying backwards and forwards ahead of us seemed swallowed in the waves. At noon we passed a Clan liner – and to all appearances it found the westward course no easy matter, since it pitched and tossed like any fishing boat. As a result of the roll, most of us felt rather seedy. A weight pressed on my chest when I rose, only to be tossed lightly across the cabin as the ship heaved heavily to our side. (I can't remember whether it is starboard or larboard.) Then the depression developed; shaving was only possible with the aid of a safety razor and, by breakfast, all appetite had gone from me. I wondered whether breakfast should be risked. The tables were being set with bars to keep the dishes in place when the ship rolled; and I decided to risk food if only to have the experience of taking food under such conditions. It was the best course – breakfast bucked me up and enabled me to put in a good many hours sleep today. But we were a subdued crowd and no sooner were we in our places than a heavy

lurch sent the dishes careering down the table. Dé had been courageous, but that roll did for him: he lay back in his seat, pushed away his plate and looked miserable. To add insult to injury, the waiter proffered him the menu, wishing to know his further orders. But all the while his lips smiled at poor Dé.

Yet, despite all internal misgivings, we were glad at heart. Surely no submarine could be active in such a sea – and even if it could be on the surface to attempt its deadly work, surely the tossing waves would carry the torpedo away from us.

November 23rd

All on board are rather nervy today. The narrow part of the Mediterranean has to be negotiated and rumour has it that the submarines have been active in this neighbourhood recently. The storm of yesterday has subsided, but the sea has by no means returned to a state of glassy calm. A stiff breeze was blowing and, in happier times, this would be an ideal day on board ship. The splash of a few waves over the deck would have added to the general exhilaration. We talked in subdued tones at meals – each might be our last. None of them were – none of us expected they would be – but one must talk about something and, at times, such grave conversations aid one's optimism. Games, such as they were, fell flat and, after the notice requesting passengers to make no mention of Wednesday's incident in their epistles was put up, letter-writing was not so feverish or general as last week when we were approaching Gib. Probably we shall be allowed to land at Malta and PCs from that island will more than serve the purpose of many rather vague and deceitful letters.

Dark came down early, and the moon was high in the sky by teatime. At 3.30 De Kretzer and Shearer coming off the watch reported unusual alertness on the bridge, dragged Staig and Dé from comfortable naps in their bunks, and gave us a most uncomfortable half hour of uneasy expectations while we watched our Escort crossing and re-crossing before our bows and signalling to us by flags. What could these flags signify? We could but wonder.

A little after tea we noticed an unusual gathering of lascars in the fore part of the ship. They were quiet but talking in excited whispers. One advanced and began tapping at the side of the ship, until a gateway swung open. Round this the crew surged and craned their necks over the sides. Then in the centre of the crowd we saw a long white bundle – and we knew what was happening. On Wednesday one of the crew had been overcome by heart failure at the time of the submarine attack, and he had subsequently died; and this was his burial. In normal times the ship would have stopped until the body was dropped into the sea, but with danger around that could not be.

Slowly the white burden was lifted over the side and slowly, inch by inch, it was lowered until it reached the waves. Then the cords were loosed, and the body disappeared from sight. All this time the moon shone down on the scene with its cold, even chilling, relentless light. When the gate was being closed again there were some who thought the muffled sound of hammering that of a gun. It certainly was very like it.

Tonight the moon was most glorious – shining clear and bright over the sea – and although we wished for no such radiance, we had comfort in that we had been told by an officer going to Gib that in France one is pretty safe during the night time when only fifty yards off from the best marksman amongst the enemy. The moonlight and the darkness are most deceptive.

Early dawn is said to be the most dangerous time in the day – we shall not be in Malta before then, but we ought to be approaching it. We ought to be nearing safety.

November 24th
Saturday, and how typical of that day which ends a week, when after a spurt of energy, one cleans oneself and then does not know how to employ the hours.

In the early morning it was impossible to open the porthole for fear of the waves dashing in: but before breakfast we had come to anchor. Desai said he did not recognize the harbour which five years ago he had arrived at in Malta: but it was Malta sure enough. There had been a fierce storm raging during the night and all day the wind was gusty and strong. Perhaps it was owing to the storm that the *Sardinia* came to this harbour – perhaps it was because the channel was not cleared of mines. When we arrived another boat, the *Nile*, was in the bay, but in a short time it left. News that Malta was reached soon spread – and everyone turned up in shoregoing togs. Some had to disembark, but as the hours passed it became evident that we would have to remain here this day at any rate. Some stir was caused by the Naval Commandant who came aboard and whose temper had been very much shortened by the *Sardinia's* lack of gangway. His language was terse and bad. The bay in which we lie is at the South end of the island and is fairly spacious. Two forts guard its extremities, and in the centre where a promontory jutting out gives two additional and more secluded havens there is an old castle. The rocks of the coast are very light coloured sandstone, and chalk. To the East the stratification is perfect – the sort of stratification which is used to illustrate geology textbooks – and on the ground above, which is gently sloping, there is a series of dry stone dykes, one above the other. These look old and may be entrenchments of former days, but I can't tell.

All the houses, and there is a fair number of them to be seen, either scattered on the main part of the island or clustering round the harbours, are of sandstone, and under the strong light of the sea their colour is very soft and warm. There does not seem to be any high land on Malta, and from the deck what panorama there is reminds me of the pictures of towns of Palestine, built in sandy places, which illustrate family Bibles.

And now for the fort – which is right opposite our porthole. It is built on some very rugged sandstone and is of sandstone itself. In shape it is like an enlarged model of the castles which make plasticine a joy eternal to children of all ages – and, seen with the sun glinting upon it and the rock on which it stands, it looks like some gigantic sand castle.

November 25th
We were all so sure of being allowed on shore that ten odd passengers in spotless raiment appeared at breakfast. The news that yesterday's short-tempered Naval Commander had been aboard with orders for us to proceed to Valetta whenever a channel was cleared (of mines presumably) spread rapidly. But the morning sped by and no movement was made. Soon there came hurrying into the shelter of the bay seven or eight large ships. Submarines were busy outside, and to go to Valetta was dangerous; however if the boats went in single file and properly escorted, the passage might be managed. One of the boats which arrived, the *Ogono of Bella*, put herself right across our stern, and serious damage was only averted by inches. The best part of an hour was spent in getting both ships into the proper distance from one another. Then at lunch the *Sardinia* moved away – and going on deck we watched the passing of the Maltese coasts and on our left the fast patrol boats protecting us from marine dangers. Just before we arrived at Valetta the news came round (with what truth I can't say – but given on the authority of a naval officer) that one of the submarines had

been captured, while the other had disappeared.

I can hardly give you an idea of Valetta. This little pamphlet may show you the lie of the island, but conveys nothing of the numerous inlets which open off the Grand Harbour and the Marsamusetto Harbour. Opposite the Custom House standing on a promontory between two inlets is the Fort St Angelo – while on the inlets of the Marsamusetto Harbour is St Paul's Bay (there seemed to be ancient ruins near here, but I had no time to investigate). *Vide* Acts of the Apostles. All along the side of the Marsamusetto Harbour there are steep rocks, and in places these have been cut into ladders and landing places. But their principal use has been as the foundation for fortifications. Fort upon fort has been reared upon these rocks – even from the ship the various layers of masonry could be traced, although often it was very difficult to distinguish where masonry began and rock ended, so huge were the stones, and so finely faced was the rock. Malta is a famous place for churches. These result from the religiosity of the people and from the connection of the Island with the Knights of St John of Jerusalem. The chimes of mellow cathedral bells greeted us as we entered the harbour. Down the road by the waterside, making a brave splash of brilliant colour against the sandy rock, were some wounded Tommies in their blue hospital coats. The progress to the quay was gradual, and in one of the harbours amongst a crowd of 'converted' tramp steamers was a wreck, the bulge of the body and a mast showing above water.

When at last we realized that the ship had stopped, we found crowds of boats waiting and hovering round her sides. First the passengers bound for Malta had to be dealt with, and when tea time had nearly arrived, the Police officer was ready to visa our passports. Simultaneously a card was stuck up stating that the boat would leave at 12 noon tomorrow. So whatever is to be done t'were well it were done quickly. Bolting a sort of tea, I was pacing the deck with Desai waiting for the others. Staig lost patience after one second and went by himself to do the town. The charge for a boat ride of about 100 yards – a most delightful row, for the motion of these modified gondolas is pleasant – was 6*d*. a head, and we were delivered from the boat to the tender mercies of one dozen gharri-drivers, two dozen guides (all more or less official and all pretty ignorant of the English language), and countless begging urchins. One of them was commissioned by Shearer to show us the way, and he pointed out such interesting places as the English Camp (we could see tents and British Tommies) the

Malta Railway (we could see the railway bridge and railway lines) and he told us where the railway lines went. He told us a gate was a gate, and that the peculiar umbrella-like black shawl of the Maltese matrons was worn by the ladies of no other place. He told us that a procession of girls in pink gingham check dresses of the most abominable cut (if any at all) and black straw hats were girls without relations in the world and 'were looked after by some sisters'. He told us the first town we came to was Floriana, and led us by the church of St Publius – the first Maltese Martyr – to a square dotted over with large weird moveable stones. This was the Granary, which had held supplies for twenty years. He shepherded us by the Mayco gardens to the Porto Reale, and so into Valetta and its main street, the Strada Reale (royal). One can't call a street High Street in Malta – that would be a bad joke, when one roadway may be fifty feet above the level of the next. The Opera House was the first building he showed us: 'Would we like tickets?' Personally I had a desire to hear Italian opera in Italian and I believe it was very good, but the others were having none. 'Would the gentlemen like postcards?', and he quickened his steps. 'This building is the signal station. It was once Spanish and is now used by the English.' Its history was, I later noticed, inscribed on a corner of the building. 'And there is the shop – Malta lace, postcards, everything.' Well, purchasing and writing messages took up some valuable time and the daylight was fleeing.

When we were ready – the moon was already high in the sky – he showed us the view from some Gardens. Below us was the Saluting Battery commanding the Grand Harbour, and beyond it was the Fort of St Angelo. Lights had appeared in all the houses, far beneath us, and the gondola boats with lamps hung on to their back, flitted to and fro and the waters reflected them. It was a wonderful sight. Next we had to see the Malta Elevator – it seemed to tremble with each breath of air. Guides do not allow for ecstatic appreciation of the view, and so onwards to the Post Office, where another importunate crowd awaited us. We were suffered to reach the Strada Reale once again, were allowed to peep into a packed church, and were hustled through the crowd again. To the right, if we could see it, was the Cathedral, and this led to the Public Library and a café. Then to the neighbouring building, which was the Governor's Palace, and the one opposite the Hotel de something or other used as a Soldiers' Club now. The Marsamusetto steps were in that direction and what would the gentlemen like to see? It was dark and the gentlemen could not see much, so we dismissed him – very handsomely rewarded – and trusted to our own bumps of location.

I would have dived into side streets, but the others thought they were shady because they were old, and we wandered rather aimlessly over our old tracks. Shearer is most fatuous when out. He cannot see anything! and ran against Staig. At last, after more wandering, Staig and Desai returned to the boat for dinner. Shearer and De Kretzer went their own ways and Dé and I saw what was to be seen. We had coffee in a funny place, where the milk was goat's milk, taken fresh from the beast, and the coffee was served in tumblers. We went down a long street past numerous old houses, through the open doors of which we saw Maltese life, and for a change went into the pictures. They were very good considering, and at about 9.00 we turned our steps towards the Marsamusetto Steps. Down a long narrow lane ending in a flight of stairs we went, and found ourselves facing the sea. Above us was the town, and when we had taken a wrong turning we found ourselves wandering among the remains of the old strongholds. The walls were massive, gigantic as the rocks, and the pathways were constructed on the model of the Maze at Hampton Court. The moonlight casting queer shadows made us feel pygmies beside these monuments of past ages. Hardly a soul was to be seen. There were ruins around us, and here and there a tiny graveyard. So we wandered on, talking of gruesome spirits who drive mortals over cliffs to certain death, and of the might of the builders of old. A half-drunk sailor led us astray, and we returned to Floriana. A sentry here put us on the track again, and, after one or two failures, we struck the road leading to the quay. It led through two ancient sally ports, of huge dimensions and deep black shadows – eerie places at night time, when one knew nothing of them. Having reached the water we were all right; a boat with a lamp bore us to the *Sardinia* and brought us back to discuss the events of the evening with Staig and Desai. Shearer and De Kretzer had not returned! It was evident that we were all marked people. Even in the darkness wretches had begged to show us the way to the *Sardinia* and gharri drivers asked leave to take us to the boat. I forgot to mention the goats. I saw no cows but flocks of goats were being driven homewards when we were coming in to Valetta – and the tinkle of their bells of various tones sounded most melodious! I was glad to find a picture of the goats in the little book of Malta views.

29

November 26th

Boat to start at 12 noon. I was up betimes – and Desai, though he tried, couldn't accompany me on shore as he had promised. Heard that a Clan liner had been sunk off Malta yesterday and that the submarine was not captured but destroyed (rather more likely). I forgot to mention that in the shop where the purchases were made last evening the man, in trying to induce the sale of real (of course!) Malta lace, said there was no danger of anything being lost through submarines. They had not been in the country for a long time. What irony!

Wherefore, I sallied forth myself, and attached myself to a tiny man whom Desai had called 'He of the waxed moustaches'. He had been in Malta – twenty years ago – and his remembrance was naturally hazy! Once again a crowd of beggars and guides awaited us and it was only by appearing like men acquainted with the place that we shook them off. Time was precious, so we had to see the sights in a hurry. First the Cathedral of St John – nothing very startling on the outside, yet with a quiet impressiveness. The interior was gorgeous. All the walls were covered with florid relief work, cupids and quaint animals in gilt. The floor was inlaid with mosaic memorials of dead Masters of the Order. The Altarpiece was magnificent, finely adorned, and I liked the figure of St John. The ceiling was decorated in the style popular in the reign of Louis Quatorze – angels in purple robes that would have served as no protection against cold winds and would have encumbered their movements through the air. Brawny soldiers in Roman arms, matrons in gorgeous dresses, and clouds of white against skies of deep light blue, which last are certainly visible in Malta. Yet in this setting these pictures looked magnificent. Round the aisles were little chapels with famous paintings, some good and some bad. There was a copy of Fra Angelico's Annunciation and two Madonnas in Byzantine work, brought from Rhodes *circa* 1560. In these only the face, very sweet and womanly, was visible, the rest of the picture being adorned with embroidery or silver and, projecting from both, came two huge crowns. We were shown the Gates of Silver, and the models of the Golden Candlesticks belonging to the English Knights. Napoleon, when in Malta, had appropriated everything with an historical, artistic and intrinsic value, had shipped them to France and thereby had been the means of losing these precious things. The ship which bore them was lost.

The caretaker took us down the Crypt, a tiny place where lie buried some famous people of whom we had never heard. It was a strange place, with stones unwrought; but by the aid of a little colour, and some lines of black paint, the suggestion of an elaborately carved crypt was given. I hardly liked the idea – remembering Ruskin on this topic. At the doorway the usual crowd assailed us – but we persevered to the Governor's Palace and through beautiful courtyards to the Armoury. The Damascenery on the Arms was past belief – exquisite was the word – but only an expert could appreciate it. Napoleon's Coronation Carriage (very uncomfortable too!) was more interesting, but a torpedo which had failed to do its duty against one of our ships in some action off Malta on 27th August of this year was the best item in the collection. It was satisfactory to see what had passed us by on Wednesday. The Council Chamber, with remarkable Gobelin tapestries representing the Continent with their flora, fauna and human species, was shown to us. It was highly necessary that a guide explained what each tapestry represented. We could never have guessed. Here the Legislature of Malta, composed of equal numbers of elected and nominated members, meets every Saturday afternoon.

Time called and, after buying a newspaper, still wet from the press because we had to clamber up numerous stairs to a printing room for it, we retraced our steps to the ship, noting the peculiar Maltese architecture – flat houses with finely wrought balconies and exceedingly heavy doors, some of these iron-studded. We had a second glimpse of the Grand Harbour, this time by daylight, and it was almost as beautiful as and more interesting than when seen by moonlight.

The hour and a half before lunch was dawdled away. There were no signs of an early start, and after lunch it was given out that the boat would not start till midnight. More shore for me! The man with the waxed moustaches had been very careful of returning in time (he gave us half an hour to spare) and told a lurid story of a man who had gone ashore at Malta and had returned to find the ship moving off. The day was stormy and, although he pulled off hurriedly, he missed the pilot boat by inches! He called on the Captain to stop but that gentleman kept on with his business. To crown the tragedy the man's wife was on board and for some time had to go husband-less. Wherefore we were in plenty of time.

None of our crowd were caring for the shore (sleep was preferable) so I attached myself to another party of an Edinburgh man and a Naval Officer. We were bound for Notabile (*vide* Guide). We took the train outwards. It is a curious means of travel – part of the way it is like an underground in mid-air, but later it comes to open country and crawls.

31

From the windows we could see how every square inch of soil is made use of. It is terraced and walled and carefully turned over, but in many places the bare rock crops through and over the whole island the soil can be only a few inches deep, if that. Prickly pear, potatoes, cabbages and maize are the chief crops. Oh yes! when going to the railway we saw the granaries being used, and much grain being taken from them for distribution and, wonder of wonders, some Maltese labourers hard at work.

Notabile is the old Capital, and is situated on a hill some distance inland. At the station three men offered to show us the way. This is one disadvantage of coming in a slack time – the supply of tourists is not equal to the demand of the guides for them. We suffered from a superfluity of them. They ran beside us, showed us where to go – and we went in the opposite direction. Tho' they understood English, they had never heard the words 'Go Away', no matter the aspect of the speaker. If we dodged them round one corner, they waited for us at the next. They drove us round Civita Vecchia back to Notabile – and when at last we took refuge in the Cathedral, one of them admitted himself and waited for us while the glories of the place were being displayed. Surely Cain killed Abel because he had offered to conduct his brother over the Garden of Eden and point out from the authorized guidebook the way of virtue. In the sanctuary of the church our thoughts towards the Maltese were very sinful. But patience and persistence achieved their object and, lest we fall prey to other guides, a crowd of whom was gathering when we left the Cathedral, we engaged him: and we were well rewarded, for his presence saved us from his fellows. Should any pitiful child look at the kind gentlemen and ask them to bless their outstretched hands, he swore at them in vigorous Maltese, and bade them leave the Signors in peace.

We were shown over the Cathedral by an ascetic looking man, whose breath stank of garlic, and he had a most appalling habit of whispering interesting things right close to one's nostrils. It seems this is the third Cathedral on the same spot, the first being small and with pillars of marble. One had been spared from the General Desolation – as a sort of memento. The second had been grand but for some reason or other part of it had been destroyed and the third Cathedral, now nearing completion, had been undertaken. It was a vast building, gorgeously decorated with bright frescoes. The church was being decked for the Xmas decorations and the choice carvings were covered, but we were shown the exquisite blendings of Egyptian marble and lapis lazuli on the Altar, the fine carving and inlay work on the choir seats, etc. etc. Napoleon had been busy rifling this place also, and the erstwhile Gates of gold and silver were replaced by replicas in brass. 'All, all,' the custodian sadly said, 'is imitation.' There were some very fine altarpieces; most were old, but one, very fresh and vigorous, was the work of a modern Italian artist. The Annunciation was the subject – and the Angel Gabriel seemed to give forth a silvery light, before which even Mary hung her head. I had an idea that D.G. Rossetti's picture had inspired this one. And one thing else. There was a portrait of the Virgin by St Luke, so valuable that every bit except the head was covered with silver for protection. St Luke must have studied in the schools of Byzantium.

The Cathedral is enormous. It will hold 3,000 people easily – the population of Notabile, priests, beggars and cultivators, is no more than 500. But Notabile is the seat of the Cardinal Archbishop of Malta – hence the grandeur. Issuing from its portals our heads were bewildered by facts about St Paul and St Publius. He was 1st Bishop, 1st Martyr of Malta, and had inspired many a native artist to feats of religious luridness, for he was torn to death by the lions at Rome. The Guide took us to the View – across the island to St Paul's Bay (not the place I had been shown yesterday) and pointed out the Musta Church. Then through the solid old gates in the massive walls of Notabile to Civita Vecchia and the Catacombs.

There are a series of these – we saw the Catacombs of the Diva Agatha. A fat old man lit candles for us and gave us into the safe keeping of his little son, who was nimble, had a gift of the gab and knew how to use his wonderful eyes. The Catacombs were used partly as dwelling places. Beds suitable for Pa, Ma and the baby, rough-hewn from the stone, were pointed out. Cooking places, hiding places, all were there. There must have been about two thousand graves in these caves, but the dead had been removed and the skulls used in the construction of the Chapel of Bones. The boy told us tarradiddles about the Phoenicians and Saracens living here – as if the Saracens would dwell in caves when houses were to be had for the plundering – and showed us fragments of 'heathen idols' which were sculptured, perhaps for some religious house, not more than three hundred years ago. A blocked up passage led to Valetta, seven miles off – and the urchin delighted in a yarn of six men and a boy being lost and perishing in a lower series of catacombs which, since that accident, had been shut up. He stamped his foot on the rock to prove it was hollow. None of the passages was over four feet high, and they were narrow and airless, despite the occasional ventilation holes. Steps were made at the most inconvenient places and, after scrambling about for some twenty minutes, I realized why the fat old stiff caretaker had sent his nimble son to act a guide. We were then led to the prison. The entrance to this was two feet square – and was so constructed, according to the youngster, to make the captives fight with one another until they died. Thro' lack of oxygen the poor souls must have been incapable of any exertion after quarter of an hour in their enforced lodging. The little kid showed all his teeth and rolled off this carefully prepared joke as he stuck the candle into the prison hole – 'Suitable place for Kaiser!' Right gladly did we welcome the return to the upper air – *Facile descensus Uomo* – and sniffed it vigorously.

Time was pressing and we had a hasty glance over the Church of St Peter and St Paul, another huge edifice with further pictures of these apostles in the Act of Martyrdom – and all done by Maltese artists. It was, however, very fine. A long broad stairway led to St Paul's Grotto. Here he had lived and preached for three months after the shipwreck. Perhaps, owing to the incident of the viper, perhaps through the faith of the believers, certain it is he was assigned the best cave or grotto. It was possible to stand upright in it, and to move freely. Here too was the first church in Malta, hidden away under the castle, and two shrines – one to St Paul and the other to St Luke – had been constructed in this cave. The statues of the Saints were by Maltese artists, and of one block of marble. A candle was placed behind the stone to show its perfections. Although it was the best cave that Paul lived in, I should have had grave objections to following his example – stuffy and smelly the place seemed to me. In order for the better exploitation of sightseers, the passage linking St Paul's Grotto with the Catacombs of St Agatha was stopped up. We had to pay twice to see what was really only one sight. Outside the Church had been a graveyard, from which the bones had been removed, and the pious Maltese had set up memorials showing the dead emerging from flames – a choice chaste thought!

A train left Notabile at five, but as we hastened down the road to catch it, we changed our minds and, after some haggling, took a gharri into Valetta. The fare was as dear as a taxi to the Waverley – and it brought us to the City five minutes after the train. The drive in the moonlight was glorious. We had a better opportunity of surveying the country – its densely populated area and the number of enormous churches. In Valetta at tea we found there were Government restrictions on eatables as at home, and after a few purchases returned to the ship for dinner.

I was slightly stiff with my unwonted exertion and I was bubbling over with details and descriptions at the table. Some folk are unenterprising to believe that two hours of sleep equalled the joys of seeing Notabile!

November 27th

Day fine. We left Valetta at 9.20 this morning escorted by Destroyer 23. After the island was lost sight of, the passengers settled down to a few days of boredom. I read, and wrote up the diary and in the evening had a talk with the doctor, who pricked the bubble of the rumour about the sinking of the Clan liner. He also informed me that the forts which Dé and I had thought were of prehistoric antiquity were 'geologically speaking' (and in such a spot which has had civilized inhabitants since the beginning of time one must speak in geological epochs) very modern. Alas for my imaginings, but at any rate they were a few centuries old and very impressive. Just as twilight fell there was a fine display of lightning on the Northern horizon. Beautiful and strange on this quiet night!

November 28th

Day passed pretty much as yesterday. I read what I had written in the diary, and was inspired by a brilliant description of the Catacombs as magnificent rabbit warrens cut out of the rock and in which men took the place of rabbits. The heat is beginning to be felt and a lassitude, especially in the afternoon, is very visible.

November 29th

Day passed as the last except that, instead of re-touching the description of Malta, I wrote a letter or two, wondering all the time that Xmas should be so near. The weather seems so unsuitable! The evening was perhaps the most perfect that I have seen at sea. The moon was at the full and its radiance actually filled the heavens. It was quite possible to read in the unshadowed places of the deck. The unusual beauty of the night seemed to have brought out all the passengers to promenade round the deck before dinner. At times the spaces were so congested that one was prevented from advancing by others coming in the opposite direction. There was another sweep today in which I did not join.

November 30th

I thought to spend today as the two previous with perhaps the addition of some feverish letter-writing, but everything has not been plain sailing. Before breakfast there was an announcement of boat drill for 10 o'clock. Evidently something was in the air, and the Steward informed us that, as we were in one of the worst parts, it had been thought desirable to have us prepared. Perhaps we had been neglectful of life-saving jackets these past two or three days. Conversation at breakfast was, therefore, suitably hushed. At 9.30 Desai and I, sitting scribbling in the companion, overheard the pale young Curate making some remarks about a submarine, and one of the ship's officers exclaiming, 'Thank God we are out of its reach now.' Such news could not be kept to oneself, wherefore we went off to build theories upon it and share it with Staig. We had just broken the news when there was one whistle. We rushed for our cork things. Was it merely the drill and signal for it? I had left mine unattended in the companion at a place where it could be very easily attacked. In about a second later the whistle blew vigorously about ten times, and everybody was rushing to the deck. I retrieved my cork thing, but by the time I reached the deck Staig was there, coated and jacketed and all prepared, looking very fierce at the sudden alarm. Shearer was down in an instant. He had been on watch and had seen the periscope. He had given the alarm and wondered why we had not been torpedoed since the periscope was seen only 800 yards off. We had not been assembled for minutes when the 'all clear' signal was given. It was remarkably quick after the alarm – so quick that there was scepticism as to the truth of 'all clear'. De Kretzer it was who had seen the real thing in the waves, and brought Shearer to make sure. There it was and it disappeared. When the Bridge was informed the officers were inclined to be rather disbelieving but, on the application of telescopes to the eyes, they were satisfied and sounded the alarm. Shearer and De Kretzer said there was slackness on the Bridge. Now why, also, had the destroyer not spotted it? Theory replied that, owing to the position of *Sardinia*, the destroyer would be out of view of the submarine and, at first, neither would see the other: When the submarine accidentally popped up its head and saw *Sardinia*, it saw no destroyer. When it came to the surface a second time the destroyer was visible so, taking thought for itself, it disappeared again into the deeps. Reflection on the courage of submarine crews followed. Day was therefore spent in writing letters home – Xmas letters too: and it closed very early at about 4.15. The moonlight was magnificent, but too clear for comfort.

There was a horrid story going about that there was no submarine seen this morning – only a pole.

1. Why should periscopes be painted red? To contrast with the blue waves.

2. Why should 'all clear' signals be given so quickly?

3. The Gunner says it was only a piece of wood.

We decided not to discuss these matters, but sleep over them.

December 1st

We have arrived at Port Said. It was in sight from 7.30 p.m. onwards – until the clock was advanced one hour, so that we be up to time. The truth of the submarine came out. It was wreckage. The destroyer, by circling round it, had made certain of that, but since the Captain had been informed by wireless of the presence of a submarine in these parts we had not been the only people deceived. Anyhow it was best to take no chances.

When we had anchored and learned that we could get on shore there were great preparations. One and all wished to be natty in whites or light things for Port Said. And what a place to be natty in! From the deck the forest of masts was a glorious sight, especially as it proved how our shipping had triumphed over the enemy's craft. There were many ships of our own and allied navies – and when we passed the *Kaiser* and *Hind*, taking a rest before setting out to dare the Mediterranean, we could not help waving them Bon Voyage.

After lunch we set out, Staig, Desai and myself, and from the little boat that took us to the landing stage we had a better view of the battleships, especially of *Monitor* with its wide spreading bottom, its huge guns and its curious single mast with an outlook stage. There was also another battleship with a similar bottom, that bristled with guns visible and with guns concealed – really a sailing fortress. The boatman made us stump up what was double the charge – but in comparison with the fare at Malta he earned his money.

There was more than the usual fuss over examination of passports and we found ourselves in dirty narrow streets with cheap-jack buildings on either side and a very variegated crowd, consisting of Arabs (in fezs and long nightgowns and elastic-sided boots, when they wore boots), French, Italians and a few English people. French seems the predominant tongue. Some notices were in three languages, but

37

the majority were in French and Arabic only. Some Arabs offered to guide us, but they were not as persistent as the Maltese. One little urchin ran up and tried to shove a French paper into our hands, crying, 'English papers – new edition – good news – War finish.' But we were not having any.

There is nothing to be seen. When in Port Said one buys postcards, writes messages home, goes to the PO where there is a waiting room, and very helpful officials who make the purchase of stamps as interesting as buying ties and, besides, are very willing to tell strangers their way about the place. Then refreshments are sought after. We wanted ices, and after one or two attempts, struck a place that advertised them, but on asking for these delights were informed that this is winter. But we could have tea and cakes. We weakly assented. The cakes were brilliant in colour, and quite barely digestible and the tea was no better. We took one cup each and then called the manager. He came and was profusely apologetic: the boy had put the tea into a pot used for making coffee without washing out the coffee grains. But we were not having any fresh tea made and contented ourselves with some fizzless tasteless lemonade.

Thereafter we strolled along the breakwater – two and a half kilometres long or, to be English, one and a half miles long. We admired the Lesseps statue commanding the harbour – about the only thing there is to admire – and saw the fishers dragging in nets. The sailing

Latest news ''The Allies Victory''

V Manavian
1916

A postcard from Port Said.
A boy attempted to sell papers to us, saying, 'Good Luck War Finish'

38

boats with bulging gaily-decked sails were interesting. Staig and Desai now left me to wander where I liked – they wanted the ship. I strolled along the beach and into the Native Quarter. Houses, even fair-sized ones, are hopelessly jerry and there is no plan in their arrangement. The sea front was monopolized by bathing machines and a camp and, tiring of these, I went down a side street and into the slums. The smells there are of the most ancient and pungent order combined with the whiffs of modern science. The natives are dirty, messy and noisy, and dress half in their old fashioned garb and half in European fashion. Cocks and cats (very lean ones!) wander about the streets, and there are sometimes fights between the two species. The houses – wooden erections put up in 1810 – are now not fit for the stabling of barrows, far less for the inhabitation of human beings, but the Arabs thrive in them and many a woman, carefully veiled, peered from their doors. Some of the women do do their marketing, but as often as not the husband made the purchase from the dirty stalls. At one place I saw a peeled onion flourishing amidst the cakes, at another a woman feeling all the rolls, and comparing their sizes before she bought. Long sticks of sugar cane about five feet long with tufts of leaves at the end were being chewed by almost every native. The more respectable cut little bits of the cane and ate these, but the others broke off the leaves and began at the top and worked their way steadily downwards.

Only one thing beautiful I saw – a sunset over the Canal and that, with the ill-smelling black market in the foreground, the gorgeous colours in the sky, and the boats on the Canal, was remarkably fine. Darkness having set in, Port Said became a place of abominations. Men stopped you and asked to conduct you to the dames and, owing to an air raid some months ago, there was so little light and the paving was so bad, that walking was positively dangerous. So I returned to the *Sardinia* for dinner and learned that Shearer and De Kretzer had made some purchases and had been grossly swindled in the transactions. The Port Said people are a set of the vilest swindlers in the world. I paid my boatman as much as he deserved – which was more than the recognized fare – but I relieved myself of a lot of bad money passed on to me in the town, so my generosity was not noble.

The evening was fine, but we had not left at 10.00 as the notice first intimated.

December 2nd

Sunday. I was awakened by the singing of Arab coolies in the ship anchored next to the *Sardinia*. Perhaps the song was some native hymn, but I hardly think so. The men were happy and clapped their hands as they sang. Certainly the Arab loves noise, and as he works he chatters incessantly. He is like a human bee – buzzing all the time he bears his burden – but he is not as active as the bee, and the taskmaster is as necessary today as when the children of Israel were in Egypt.

We left Port Said at about 8.00 and entered the Canal as breakfast began. There were some changes: one or two new passengers – some naval officers who were in command of a lot of sailors going to Bombay. These sleep anywhere on deck, and everybody envies them. The stewards and all the crew had on whites – looking very clean indeed, but the smell of laundry which dispelled the charm of the evening is not so pleasant, tho' a necessary consequence of the change.

Ships are only allowed to go through the Canal at a rate of 5 miles per hour – so starting at 8.00 we arrived at 10.00 p.m. Crawling thus along we had a splendid view of the banks, which at present are most interesting. The West Bank, for most of its length, is tree covered and, although there is only a strip of green, it was most refreshing to gaze upon. Great changes have been made there within the last two years. Roads (very good) have been constructed its whole length. When interest waned on one side one could turn to the other. The camp of Cantara was on the Eastern Bank. It stretched for miles in length and breadth. Here the Turks had tried to break through but without success: and now it serves as a base (for a railway has been constructed) for Palestine. As we passed, bales of grass were being unloaded from ships into lighters and from these again taken ashore. Whole stacks of these could be seen lining the bank. Yet for all the activity no one appeared to be very busy. Once an aeroplane flew overhead and descended some distance ahead of us. Mules there were in plenty dragging little trucks – when the stick was sufficiently applied: and the Arabs in their long robes (most cumbersome garb) seemed to find life one long game. At one station there were rows and rows of donkeys waiting to be driven across a pontoon after we had passed.

There was a service this afternoon. I played the piano in the companion which acted as a sort of organ loft above the Saloon where the service was held. It was very fine, especially as all the sailors were paraded for the Church and sang lustily. In the evening again I had more hymn playing: a sort of hymn song affair in the 2nd Saloon. The sailors all turned out, and after the Clergyman gave out a hymn – to start the proceedings – they were asked to choose what they wished, and they tumbled over one another in their eagerness. That was a busy and a very hot hour. Outside the air was chilly, very chilly, after the heat of the afternoon – 80 degrees in the shade. The Naval Officer in command is musical and is going to organize a Naval Concert before Bombay is reached. Some stunt!

The afternoon was very hot and sleepy and the Canal banks were most uninteresting until we came to Ismailia, at the head of Lake Tinifrek, at about teatime. Here again the Turks had attacked the Canal. Deserted engines of quaint antique shape, because of their narrow gauge were left to rust and decay. Sandbags and wire entanglements were still visible on the East Bank. Seven months ago, I was told, there was a continuous guard of soldiers – down to Ismailia – and now there were only a few, and these were bathing in the Lake. Ismailia is a Mohameddan town situated near a belt of trees, but it is not very exciting looking. Again there was more Canal proper – sand on one side and trees on the other – until we came to the Bitter Lakes, where the course is marked by buoys and stationary ships. Towards 10.00 we approached Suez. A busy string of twinkling lights was what we saw first, then they broadened and the town spread before us. It seemed neat, trim and well-kept, but the darkness was favourable to it. Nearing the end of the Canal we had to drop the pilot who had steered us thro' and, since he took an inconceivably long time leaving, I went to bed after a last look round – when mountains on either side loomed through the night.

All day the thought that the PO had sent the telegram telling of my safe arrival at Port Said cheered me, and I often wondered what everyone was doing. Egotistically I pictured No. 2 London Street as a scene of feverish epistolatory activity, and that I was to be the recipient of the results of that energy. It was, however, good to think of.

December 3rd

I was awakened in the middle of the night with the chill of the air. I was shivering as I have sometimes shivered when I had gone to bed with windows open at home and an East wind had sprung up: but the day which followed was exceedingly warm, and everyone exceedingly active. The *Sardinia* had left Suez during the night and, in our first few hours of wakefulness, we saw the mountains that border the Gulf of Suez. Rugged peaks they are – and barren – but mellowed by distance they were beautiful. Somewhere amongst them must have been Mt Sinai, where the Law came down, and somewhere in the neighbourhood the Egyptians were engulfed.

Soon we passed into open sea and turned our thoughts to amusing ourselves. An awning and a net were rigged up on the starboard side and then quoits were indulged in, and in the afternoon some practice cricket. It was hot work and, after a life of idleness, tiring.

Last night a challenge to a team of Navy men for tug o' war had been laid and accepted. The morning was spent in recruiting the passengers' team. There are several hefty men on board, and at 12.00 there was practice – good solid practice. At five the tug o' war took place. Betting was in favour of the sailors: and the deck was crowded. The lifebelt box served as grandstand, and chairs were used for standing on. Amidst huge excitement (which is the correct expression) the signal for the heaving was given. It was a long pull, a strong pull and a tough pull: often the yellow ribbon was carried now to the right now to the left of the mark. The sailors not in the pull roared themselves hoarse. It was a good pull and the passengers won. Round two, sides changed over – and this time, after a good contest, the sailors won. It was a sight to see the NCO of the Marines, timekeeper of the Naval side, giving instructions, cursings and the signal for the heave all at once. The reward of victory was to be a bottle of Bass and he seemed to be a man for whom such a prize could not be allowed to slip from his grasp.

The third round resulted in an easy win for the passengers – and so the sailors lost their beer. Perhaps the slope of the ship was in favour of the passengers, since the winning team in each round was always on this side. But it was good fun – and there is another challenge out for tomorrow.

The concert broached last night came to fruition today. One or two of the passengers helped: and through this it comes to light that a mysterious box on the starboard side contained a piano, and a very good instrument too. It was opened out for the concert, but not used. That affair was timed to start at 8 o'clock, but did not begin until 8.25. All the sailors were there – and all their talent was on the programme, which first was censored before the ladies entered. The Second Saloon at the best of times is a stuffy hole but, packed with sailors and others, it was soon in a state of hot airlessness – like an oven in fact. Part of the delay had been caused by the failure of lights, candles being a very unsatisfactory substitute. So, when all had settled, the Chairman – a

42

sailor blushing to the roots of his hair – welcomed everybody, apologized for his speech and said he intended to be pleasing. Item One – 'The Long Long Trail'. The singer had a little voice which the piano drowned, but he livened up in the chorus, which went with a gusto. Then the lights failed again and, with difficulty remembering the tune, I kept up a sort of accompaniment. I played the melody somehow, as I groped for keys in the darkness, and the chorus enjoyed itself hugely and sang ever louder and louder – 'There's a long long trail a-winding.' Candles hastily lit served to brighten up the last bar and, with the striking of the last chord and the last loud shout, the lights went up.

I had to play from sight all sorts of ragtimes, sung in nondescript keys and vamp or, at least, serve out some sort of musical background to some other songs in which no sooner had I settled down to play a certain key than the voiceless singer began to sing in one totally different. In the case of the loud man it was fairly easy. His first song was of Cowboy Jones, an eminent cinema star, whose chief accomplishment was that he gave people Hell. Naturally Hell came in the chorus, and it goes without saying that each time the chorus was repeated, Hell seemed to attract all the vocal power of the sailors. 'Give 'em Hell' continued until the officer begged for a little less Hell, but he was not heard and, when it came to be sung for the last time, its popularity beat all previous records. His second was an improved version of 'Old King Cole' in which that gay old Monarch called for many other persons besides his fiddlers and courtiers. There was his parson, his tailor and his cobbler, and somewhere in the chorus there was a 'Damn' – to make things lively. But he was really very good – acted as he sang and had a swig of soda water in the pauses of the songs. He was cheered to the echo. And there were other ditties – old things I was told without tune and sung without tone, which I could not follow and the singers could hardly remember. One concerned an Old Mill Stream where the weepy hero discovered that his beloved by the village green was not really worth loving, and that besides being beautiful she was sixteen (impossibly early age). I could not understand this reference.

I sighed when it was over, but it was followed by another old song – about him who is not a Nelson nor yet a Wellington but one of King Edward's boys – and a hero because he is a true British Working Man. Unfortunately the singer forgot the second verse, and we did not hear what happened to him. The pale young parson sang a song of Handel's (words by Congreve, concerning a bad Restoration Rake, of whom parsons should know nothing at all) and a charming gay old English hunting air, which the sailors soon took up and sang – really sang. Incidentally, the parson has given me the names of one or two books on Indian Music, which I must buy in Bombay. Another passenger sang a song which he did not know and came in always at the wrong place, while the sailor who was turning over the music also turned it over when I was not wanting it turned. But the song went down.

The concert concluded with two of Harry Lauder's, which a Mr Allen sang. He had a very good strong baritone and, being a tippler himself, entered well into the spirit of 'It's a Wee Dochan Doris'. That and 'Roaming in the Gloaming' were the two outstanding successes of the evening. They were howled and the singer, had the men had their way, would have been kept on the floor till midnight. Here the King was proposed and his health was sung and the concert finished. It was some stint – and it was hot. By the end of the first song there was perspiration all over me: and by the end of the evening I was like a turkey cock, but I liked it and am ready for another should it be wanted. The evening was fine and coolingly warm but, even so, it was an hour and a half before I was back to a normal temperature. My Word, I'm tired!

December 4th
Today passed pretty much as yesterday. I am a trifle stiff in the arms as a result of my exertions, but that stiffness must be worked off. Cricket is splendid but I am a feeble bat and bowler.

There was a singsong for the sailors tonight, again in the Second Saloon, and again I was in a great bath of perspiration. I had more enlightenment into the composition of a sailor. Certainly he likes comic songs and lively songs, but he also loves and hugs to his bosom the most feeble wishy washy sentimentality. Two brawny ABs who sent the crew into convulsions with songs which were so frank as to be very very shocking followed these up by two tearful lays about Sister Mary in Heaven, Let us pray for Sister Mary, etc. It was much freer than the other, but there is to be a programme affair tomorrow night.

I heard about the ship I mentioned at Port Said. The *Grafton* it is called and, if ships could be decorated, would have won the VC for its work at Gallipoli. It has twice been torpedoed, but still is going strong. It is a wonderful ship.

December 5th

Something has gone wrong with the engines, and we shall not arrive at Aden till Saturday. We are slowly moving down the Red Sea – one might almost say drifting down it: but we have so much to do now that we never think of the slow passage of time. There are competitions at Quoits and Bull Board. In the afternoon there was a cricket match – Passengers v. Navy – and in the evening another concert. This time it was held on the 2nd Class Deck, the sailors having unscrewed the piano of the Second Saloon and carried it upstairs. There was a good big audience and everybody was pleased with the turns. Unfortunately the star comedian had made himself so tight that he could not appear – and one or two of the more spicy items had to be omitted by request. There was a violin 'Obbligato to the Rosary' and a mandolin accompaniment to the 'Perfect Day'. What a commotion when the music of the 'Rosary' was lost. What a turning over for that piece. The concert was at a standstill – and it was only by carrying on to the next item while the search was being continued that any progress was made. Moreover the violinist's string broke. More delay, but what of that? Everybody was happy, and when some programmes were auctioned for sailors' charities about £5 10s. was raised. Not bad – but I'm a-weary, and I must off to bed.

December 6th

I signalized this morning by slicing my finger instead of the roll. The doctor, when applied to for sticking plaster, made a most picturesque job of it, with cotton wool and boracic lint, etc.

The crew had fire drill at about 10 o'clock, and this was interesting to watch. The day passed much as the preceding days unless there was more listlessness and less energy displayed. The 2nd Tug o'War – Navy v. Passengers – again resulted in a defeat for the Navy. The passengers are much bigger and heavier than the sailors, and it was found that, in order to have equality of weight, the sailors would require to be 13 to 12 passengers. The pulls were not so hotly contested as before and there was much less enthusiasm. We are still in the Red Sea. This accident in the Engine Room will delay us three days at least.

Owing to the enlarged state of my left forefinger I could not play, but the gramophone more than compensated for this omission.

45

December 7th

We ought to have been near Aden, but the confounded accident in the engine room has delayed us and, for most of the day, we were in the Red Sea. Every narrowing of the sea, every group of islands passed, was taken as the Gates of Hell and the curse known as the Straits of Babel Wand etc. In the days of wooden ships, the winds, the rocky barren coasts and the numerous island rocks made these straits a death trap. Perim and the Straits, however, were not reached until after 5.00. All day long a strong wind, almost amounting to a gale, was blowing. It retarded our progress (the day's run was only 199 miles), but it was cooling and most invigorating. There has been a rumour going around the lascars that a Rajah is on board; and Fernandez, the steward who looks after Dé, Desai and De Kretzer, called Desai aside and asked if Dé was he. Perhaps he recognized the attributes of Rajahhood in the sleeping Dé – he spends at least fourteen hours per day in bed. Perhaps he was taken with Dé's cap. At any rate he has been an ideal steward and has provided the three of them with sufficient fruit to keep us also well supplied. Such is the homage due to Royalty!

December 8th

Aden hove in sight at about 9 o'clock this morning and, mean as the town is from the ship, its situation has the grandeur of a fjord. The rocks rise from the coast to about 400 or 600 feet, and they are sharp and rugged through the weathering in a rainless atmosphere that is subject to extremes of temperature. The outline of the barren rocks of Aden recalls the famous bagpipe melody, which jerks itself up and down with every other note. On the Western side there was a similar rocky promontory garnished with one or two islands, while to the North there was a low-lying shore evidently sandy and with mountains in the distance. These may have been the result of mirage. They seemed to float in mid-air, their base rising out of some inland sea (which of course does not exist).

I had not intended disembarking because, according to the notice put in the companion, there might be some fuss but, as Desai wanted to walk, I accompanied him, and jolly glad I was that I did so. We had a ripping day. There was no fuss. Aden is part of Bombay Presidency – and ICS (Indian Civil Service) means something there. The policeman, when we were coming away, used his stick to the boat boys to make them hasten to carry out our wishes. What funny kids these boys were. Black as black, white teeth, and perpetual movement.

They are always chattering, wrangling, singing. Some of them put henna on their woolly hair to make it a peculiar brown (the natty shade in these parts).

In Aden there is nothing to see except the tanks. The main street is straggling and mean, although the shops do a good business. The merchants are chiefly Indians and many a fine fat old fellow with great gold specs we saw driving past us. Aden is a freak town. It is built on rocks and the shrubs are so rare as to be countable on the hand. There is one tree – a banyan tree – and it is by the tanks. There is no greenery except in the square round Queen Victoria's Statue and in the gardens beside the tanks. Camels are the chief native beasts of burden, small and ungainly as they are. I expect their lot is not enviable. The carts which they drag are low and long and the shafts rise to the beasts' sides at a most awkward angle. Now and again a man riding a camel with satisfaction and enjoyment passed, and once we saw an obstinate camel resting complacently by the road while its owner applied the lash and curses.

There were a number of taxis, many horse gharries and a few bullock carts. It was strange to find the most primitive and most up to date means of locomotion existing side by side. Goats were the only domestic animals, although they had no visible means of subsistence. I noticed one eating a rag – but there were many goats, and I liked goat butter when I had it at lunch.

To keep the roads cool, boys are employed to go into the sea and fill leather bags slung round their shoulders, and then to return and sprinkle the roadway. From the landing stage the tanks were a good three miles away and, with the heat of the sun and the desolate barren uninteresting nature of the landscape, it seemed longer. The road was fairly straight except at one place, where it climbed a considerable hill and led through a cutting where the rocks towered about 100-150 feet on either side of the road. Thence it took us down to old Aden, a curious place with Native Bazaar and all, and many many dirty people. Here were the Connaught Lines and the headquarters for the forces who are defending Aden. Fighting is taking place about ten miles from the town, and last July the Turks advanced somewhat closer but, shelled from British ships in the Gulf, they suffered heavily and had to retire. The scarcity of water is the chief difficulty with the Aden Campaign.

There were only a few soldiers knocking about, and one or two of these were Indians. Up on the rocks were the remains of some artistic soldier's work. It was as good as the wool work pictures done by disabled sailors on the streets. At the post office we could not get change of good English money and, feeling tired and not sure where the tanks were, we took a gharri. The tanks had been quite close, but the sun was hot and there was nothing to be gained by risks. The Chowkeedar, who looked after the place, was an Indian who spoke Hindustani. Consequently Desai gained much information from him: chiefly that there is rainfall here once every seven or eight years; that when the tanks are full, the water lasts for three years, and is sold at the rate of a halfpenny a gallon. At other times the rate for distilled water is 4*d.* a gallon. Rain had fallen in June 1915, and I could see a little of what was left. It was protected by that banyan tree, which seemed to be rooted in rocks. Beneath its shade coolies were working at a deep well drawing water for putting on a few shrubs near the tanks. The Chowkeedar was old, and said that since his boyhood they had only been filled three times.

They are of unknown date and were discovered accidentally in 1859 and have been carefully preserved. They have been formed out of a hollow basin in a cleft of the rocks by a series of dams. Channels were constructed to catch and lead every available drop of water from the rocks above. When no water was in the tanks it was easy to see where the water had been. Above, the rocks were sharp – rugged, black and angular. Below, they were rounded and smoothed as if by sea action, and they were wonderfully white. It certainly was worth while coming along the dry dusty road to see them. At the gate some beggars waited for us, and they wept and howled when they discovered us copperless.

The drive back in the gharri seemed very short, and it landed us in the square in good time for lunch at the Hotel de L'Europe. Lunch was served in a long room, the walls of which were lined with dilapidated dusty ornate sideboards. But the fare was good, and the charge moderate. After a few purchases we were returning to the boat, when an Indian stopped Desai who, at first, did not recognize the stranger. He was a cousin, Indian fashion, which is a cousin whom we would not know in all probability. When Desai left five years ago he was a little boy and now he is a mustachioed man, and something in the port trade. He wished to drive us back to Old Aden and have tea there, but since time prevented that, he took us to his friend the doctor. His house is perched on the rocks near the signal station, so as to catch every wind that blows and we rested there for an hour and had a second lunch – of Indian food. I enjoyed it very much indeed, and I think I made it evident that my enjoyment was real. From Desai's cousin and the doctor we learned one or two things about the place: that vegetables are 8*d.* a pound, and that the fighting never seems to bother anyone.

The *Sardinia* was timed to leave at 4.00 and we had a rush to be back on board at the stated hour. Desai's cousin helped us and showed us the way, and made matters smooth with the boat boys, who rejoiced to give us a good roll for our money.

On board there was a rumour that we would not start till tomorrow morning but it proved false, and we left in a hurry a few minutes before six. After 6.00 the port is closed and we should have had to remain in the harbour all night. The engine seems to be sorted so that our speed is quite normal, and we may reach India before next Saturday.

When the coolies scrambled over the sides of the ship onto a barge to take them to Aden they set up yells and cheers, and held up their hands. Pennies they wanted, and pennies they got in plenty. They seem so carefree, so contented with so little. To see their cheerful smiles and the mad scrum for an anna, was worth the coppers thrown to them. They are the most irresistible beggars I've met yet.

How glad we were to leave Aden! We felt we were at the entrance to Bombay Harbour already!

The Naval Ratings had arranged still another concert tonight. Four a week is almost too much, but this was very good. They had rigged up a stage with bunting on the second class deck: and halfway down the programme had a sketch. It was an up to date Punch and Judy Show, and was called the 'Mad Mullahs'. A Warden in an Asylum goes off for a short time leaving the place in charge of a young spark with a screw loose. As the patients come in one after another, he deals with them in the approved Punch manner. His assistant sissy comes to his aid and gives every loony a crack over the head with a cudgel and either knocks the Mad Footballer, the Mad Boxer, the Mad Fisher etc. senseless or out of this world. The final patient is a love-sick maiden who seeks her Harry, but her tonic is not administered correctly and she dies of arsenic poisoning. When the Warden returns and is threatening, as well as feeling rather queer at being responsible for all these tragedies, he too gets one on the napper – and the sketch ends with an array of bodies on the stage. It was highly amusing. The other items were more carefully prepared than previously and the mandolin solos went well. There was one great advantage which this concert had over the others – it was short, and everything was over by 10.00. After all my exertions today I am tired, and very ready for my bunk.

December 9th

Sunday. Arabia ever on the port side, seen as a faint line of blue hills upon the horizon. Africa was spotted about 5 o'clock, but soon disappeared. Everybody was on their best of behaviour. Service as usual at 10.45 a.m. and hymns at 8.15 p.m. The advent of Xmas involved the selection of numerous Xmas hymns – and the pale young curate wished all present a Happy Xmas when it came.

December 10th

We are now forging ahead across the Indian Ocean, but what of that? There is so much to occupy us that we never think of the sea. But all are concerned with the speed of the ship – 10 knots only. Probably we shall land at Bombay on Saturday afternoon – all dressed up with no place to go.

To enliven the day there were some sports, chiefly nautical, but one race, the potato spoon – for euphony called the egg and spoon – was reserved for passengers. I was thankful I was in the semi-final, and had two very exciting races. There had been a subscription made last week for these sports for the sailors, and today and tomorrow there are to be races and competitions for them. The prizes are 7s.6d. and 2s.6d. and the men will have earned the money, especially the winner of the obstacle race. They were some obstacles! The course lay over and under some hoisted ropes. The men started aft, along 2nd Saloon Deck, down to Hold Deck, up and over a rope ladder on to 1st Deck. Then there were sacks to crawl through and barrels hanging from the roof had to be negotiated. There were still more obstacles in the crew's quarters and when, at last, the men returned to the deck panting they had to crawl under tarpaulin before they reached the goal. To see the race properly one had to run with the men but, although that was impossible, it was ripping fun. I asked the Captain if I could photo and, as a result, took some snaps. I wonder with what results. The crew of natives enjoyed the sport, but could not understand what we were up to; and the monkey, when it saw the runners coming, jumped from spar to spar and rope to rope as in its native jungle. This race, and the pillow fighting, in which two men sat on a bar placed above a sail filled with water, and battered each other with pillows till one slid from the pole into the water, was a huge success. Some fifty passengers took part and they more than matched the sailors, who often tried to balance themselves by holding on to the pole. The referee had to declare three or four men out for doing so. For these two events the men turned up in their oldest things, which gaped in every inconsiderate part. Perhaps that would give them freedom of motion – but only perhaps – because even in the most frantic part of the obstacle race some men had to stop and pull their jerseys about them, so losing time.

In the forenoon the minor sports were held, such as chalking the deck (when a man was held by his foot to the roof and had to chalk the deck as far beyond a given mark as he could), potato and bucket race, cockfighting, (in which a man was trussed up by having his hands tied together below a pole thrust under his knees) and the whistling race (in which each had to eat a dry biscuit, return to the starting place and whistle a set tune before they could run to the winning post). Some of the men swallowed their biscuits whole and then, in their efforts to whistle say 'Annie Lawrie', became red in the face; unless the biscuit came out instead of the tune, they nearly choked.

It was great, but the cockfighting was better. One red-headed giant, who had sung the most banal sentimental lays at the concert and who, by profession, is a boxer or footballer, carried all before him. He would advance a few wriggles, wriggle a bit, get his toes beneath his opponents and send them spinning out of the ring. He was good at the game, but he was an ugly sinner. All the time the sailors shouted catchwords from the sketch as encouragement. To the chilling hero of that play they shouted, 'Go it Tiny,' yet Tiny was about thirty-five if a day and had an ugly leer and a gaping mouth. Or, if they were excited, they yelled, 'Give 'em Grog,' in reference to the Universal Cure-All in the Army and also to the Fail-me-never Remedy in the Sketch – a lay-out blow on the head.

These made a fine break in what would have been a day of drowsiness. The weather is more bracing, more breezy and more brilliant than any we have had. Although the temperature is nothing like as high as it was in the close heat of the Red Sea, there are more and more white things appearing daily. I shall need to have a new rigout in Bombay, which we hope to reach on Saturday morning.

December 11th
The sports continued today, and there was one sensation. The pillow-fighting semi-finals had taken place – there had been two good duckings and we were waiting for the last and best fight of all. The Passengers' strong man had his hands on the bar ready to slide along when, without warning, there was a sound of tearing. As if a dam in Holland had burst, the water poured out. It flooded the deck and the lascars on

cookers were standing knee-deep in the water. If we were disappointed for the time being not having the final when it was expected (it came off at about 5.00 when the sail had been mended) this catastrophe made up for it.

The most exciting event for the sailors was called 'Are Goin There' and consisted of two blindfolded heroes trying to hit one another's head. Not so easy as it sounds. For the passengers there was 'Chalking the Pig's Eye' and, if De Kretzer did not win the prize, his effort was the most popular. He put the eye at the wrong end of the pig. And there was a 'Threading the Needle' race – not so very easy, even with darning needles and thin thread.

In the afternoon, when the pillow-fighting was over, two of the organizers had quite a good time and gave us quite a good laugh by playing at 'Are you there?' above the water. They wanted a fine splashing, and got it. The Prize Distribution was at dusk – and the Champion was the boxer fellow. He had been knocked out in the Final cockfighting – greatly to the joy of his mates it seemed – greatly to our joy too but he had won most prizes and was rewarded as an extra prize a pipe. He is a non-smoker, so is the donor.

I had wanted to develop some films and making the cabin into a dark room involved some work. Every available rug, blanket, towel, pillow and article of clothing was used to stop up some chink of light. A red cloth was swathed round the lamp. The results, if not all I could

After the pillow fight. You may see the splash from the water in the sail

have wished, are better than I had expected for my first attempt at films.

December 12th
Still the Indian Ocean 'sets and smiles'. Without sports the day dragged, and the hours to mealtimes were counted. We had to fill up a Customs Declaration for use at Bombay, and had to state how many firearms or other weapons of destruction we were carrying ashore. I printed some of the photos. They are passable.

December 13th
Printed more photos today and watched, giving unnecessary advice while Staig and De Kretzer pack. According to the notices, we are to arrive at Bombay at 12 noon Saturday, although there is a rumour that we will arrive at Boteeted Area at 8.00 tomorrow. However, the *Sardinia* does not hurry herself: she crawls across the Indian Ocean, which is as lazy a sea as can be pictured. Day follows day and there is nought to do but sleep or grouse. A little cricket was played in the afternoon to prevent people from becoming too bloated. Some Indian Army Colonels seem to have awakened to our existence and are striving to make themselves useful to us. Rather late in the day, but one must be thankful for small mercies.

December 14th
This is to be our last full day aboard, and what hours were not spent in packing were listlessly suffered to go on their course. We took turns in littering the cabin floor with our belongings – despaired one after the other of having room in our boxes for all we had, and eventually discovered that the boxes would have held even more. Early in the morning we sighted gulls – sure sign of land somewhere near. After dinner, as is customary I believe, the Captain was toasted and thanked for having brought the passengers safely to their destination; and all stood and cried, 'Hurrah', and sang, 'For he's a jolly good fellow'. In terms of a notice put up, this jubilation was premature. Three months ago a P&O was sunk by a mine off Bombay and, although there were no casualties, no one was prepared. The lifebelts were all in safe places, not easy of access. Hence passengers were advised, for their own safety, to keep their lifebelts at hand while the minefield was being negotiated. Those who had been most fearful of submarines were most scornful of this new danger.

Just before turning in a huge hospital ship coming from Mesopotamia was sighted going India-ward. It moved slowly onwards in a blaze of lights.

December 15th

All dressed up in the morning and all packed by 10.00. We hoped to reach Bombay at noon, but even at 11.00 land was visible only as a line of misty clouds. As the minutes passed it grew in distinctness. Islands detached themselves and lighthouses came into prominence. Soon the white houses on Malabar Hill showed against the greenery; and then the towers of Bombay appeared. Beautiful they were through the mist. The biggest dome of all crowned the monster Taj Mahal Hotel – so big it was, so imposing that it seemed rather like some Government Buildings. Desai pointed out the various towers – the Senator's House – the Station – the Post Office and, as we neared the Harbour, the grandeur of the buildings could be seen. The sea had become very green and very muddy, for it is shallow. It was like an ocean of water which had been used for mixing paints. In the bay many white-sailed fishing boats sailed by, and tufts of seaweed floated along.

Meantime the heat grew ever more intense, and the sun ever more glaring. Hospital ships were anchored in the bay, to the number of five – monster boats bearing three Red Crosses on each side.

We were to go alongside the Alexandra Pier, not the Ballard Pier generally used and, in passing, saw the new P&O Pier under course of construction. When it is finished there will be but a step from boat to Railway Station – and no worry.

One lock had to be passed – a slow business when everybody was anxious for the shore and, after much twisting and turning, SS *Sardinia* at length came to her berth. Crowds of natives were awaiting the arrival and some Europeans were there too. The chattering (the noise was pleasant if one were humorously inclined) and the amount of labour and energy wasted on unnecessary jobs which had to be discussed volubly and then undone, was amusing to watch. Passports had to be examined and money changed and, to save all bother with the Customs, I told Grindlay's man to look after my luggage.

Then we disembarked and, hearing that the Secretariat was still open, drove there in a hurry through a town that seems to be in the process of construction. Heard I am posted to Bengal, as also is Staig, and have to report to Calcutta. Staig is for off but, having no cash for

Staig, Desai and De Kretzer

the journey, I have to wait with Shearer till Monday. Next ensued much tearing about Bombay in taxis and gharries, and much fuss seeing Staig's luggage through the Customs to the station and there getting a berth in the train.

As a result, when we came to seek our hotel there was darkness in Bombay and we lost our way in the Residential Quarter, where there were many spacious gardens and no kindly soul to tell us the way. So we wandered on and on, far from the Hotel, but at last finding an unoccupied gharri we were able to gain the place we sought. Here my luggage was reported as having been taken away – more anxiety, more fears – but a room for two was engaged. Spacious it is, with a high roof and two huge beds. Bathroom attached to bedroom – everything all right. We had no time to examine things.

Staig and De Kretzer were leaving in an hour – back to the station through darkened streets, and there we saw the Express Trains start. Staig and Dé were in Calcutta, De Kretzer for Colombo (via Madras) and his bride. What crowds were there – what chattering. Families with their belongings in a bundle and a brass cooking pot squatted on the station. Parsi boys went here and there as if intent on business. The third class compartments seemed bursting with the crowd of humanity, and round the doors stood almost as many as were within. Some bore garlands round their necks and bouquets in their hands. This is the true Indian fashion of welcoming or speeding the guest. Sellers of sweet sticky things passed before the train bellowing and doing a lively trade, and sellers of oranges sat and found the passengers so afflicted with qualms of thirst that they had no need to cry the merit of their wares. By 9.30 De Kretzer, Shearer and I returned to the hotel. I fumed all the way about my baggage but, when I arrived, I was told of the mistake and there it was waiting for me.

Oh! but I was tired. It was only 10 but I was between the sheets in a few minutes. From below came the sound of billiard balls – rat-tat-tat – and they sent me to sleep. The electric fan made breezes blow all round the bed, so that I seemed to rest upon the arms of a Zephyr and, so resting, I slept fairly soundly until this morning.

A voice that seemed to come out of the darkness of infinity, a voice that seemed to be crying through the mists of dawn roused me with the call of 'Sahib'. It was a faint weary call – and the Sahib was aweary also so he turned once again to his pillow, but not before realizing that he had now reached the shores of India and was indeed a man – a great man – a 'Heaven-born'.

Here endeth the journal of the Voyage to India. I had thought to continue, but could write nothing in the train and these last few days have been too crowded for literary effort. So here endeth the diary – for continuation see letters!

Memories of India in the ICS
(written in retirement)

This sheet has been facing me for nearly two years now, and I cannot any longer resist the invitation to write, but about what should I write? When one is – according to the polite phrase – a Senior Citizen, the passage of the years is far too swift and uneventful to be worth recall. Perhaps I had better try and delve into my memories of what is now called the Raj – the British Empire in India – though I know but one small corner of it called Bengal. Bengal saw the making of history in the eighteenth century but, by the twentieth, had lost most of its romance to Delhi, the Military Cantonments and the Princely States. Such memories as I shall record will not be in chronological order, but I shall always try to give dates, so that they can be related to the political atmosphere of the time. I think my memory is clear and accurate as to detail, though I can never be certain of that. I learnt in the witness box how fallible my memory could be after the lapse of a few months, not on essentials however, but on circumstances somehow connected with what was at issue. Their relevance was not great, but doubt was cast on the credibility of my evidence – to the satisfaction of the lawyer of the guilty accused.

1917-1918: First Impressions
I think I shall begin with my arrival in India – my first encounter with the East. What I had read at home had not prepared me for what I found. It was chiefly the little things that came as a surprise. Those who had relatives who had served in India knew what to expect, but never seemed to pass on their wisdom to those who had not. However well kitted out one might be by outfitters in Britain, much of what one bought for the Tropics was unsuitable and seldom used. If one heeded the advice to wait till one got to India, there was still this journey from the port to one's station to undergo before one could make real preparations for carrying on. Yet, though one was a stranger in a strange land, there was always someone ready to help and advise. One of my

57

clearest memories of those days is of the kindness to a greenhorn from men whom I met on my journey but would never see again.

Now for some facts. On leaving the ship I made straight for a hotel because I had to collect some money, and that meant spending a night in Bombay. Thus, with Staig and Shearer, I went to the Bombay Secretariat to report our arrival in India, for our Service dated from the day we stepped ashore in India and not from our departure from Britain, nor our arrival in whatever Station to which we might be posted. The voyage had taken seven weeks, and had not been without its perils, so we were not surprised to be told that rumour had been current (and believed) that the ship had been torpedoed and had sunk with all on board. The next stop was at Grindlay's to secure some cash, and arrange for the train journey to Calcutta the next day. The Bank considerately met all our demands, which were not very great, but there was trust in the Service, even for a fledgling member of it.

I felt I had been made welcome to the country and had the good wishes of the staff at the Bank, and that was most encouraging.

Bombay – Calcutta by train
We had a tour of the city, but missed all the sights we had expected, as the gharri-wallah was quite uninterested in what we wanted to see. Then Staig left for his Station and Shearer and I returned to the hotel. Next morning there was no time to go to the shops. Shearer's train left in the morning for Patna, mine in the early afternoon. To one accustomed to the crowded travel of the mainline trains between London and Edinburgh, the spaciousness of the coaches on the East-Indian train came as a surprise. I had to, or at any rate was expected to, travel first class as a Member of the ICS, and I had only ever gone third class at home. At that time there was no second class, and I don't remember there being any sleepers on the trains. At any rate, if there were sleeping coaches, they were not in evidence. If one travelled overnight one sat up in great discomfort and was grateful if one managed to doze off for a short respite. Sometimes one had to spend most of the night in the corridor. But the Indian coaches had to provide for daytime and night-time travel and for journeys of more than twenty-four hours. One of the compartments had four beds – two lower and two higher – which were raised up against the side of the coach during the day. And, of course, there were the usual toilet facilities, but without soap or towels.

Fortunately, I had only one companion for the whole journey to

Calcutta. He was a tea planter returning from leave to his garden in Assam. He was not a great conversationalist, but that was of little account, as he put me wise to the precautions to be observed when travelling by night, to ensure that there were no nocturnal intruders. He also lent me towels, pillows and soap, so that I could wash and stretch out and have a proper sleep. As there were no blinds on the windows, privacy was obtained by raising louvred shutters while lowering the windows, to prevent the compartment from becoming a stifling furnace.

There were of course no corridors so, for meals, one had to leave the compartment (trusting one's belongings would be safe) and proceed to a dining car or, as I think was customary there, to a railway station dining room or saloon. They were never thought of as restaurants. After being confined to the compartment for hours, the short walk to the refreshment room came as a relief. At some of the bigger stations, or main junctions, the food and service was quite good. At others it was sub-standard, though in the circumstances none the less acceptable.

This train journey from Bombay to Calcutta is surely the most uninspiring introduction to India. The view always seemed the same – bare parched plains with few trees, mud huts clustering together and only an occasional cow or goat looking for grass, which was not in evidence. There were no men working in the fields and, now and then, I would see a woman carrying a water jug. The absence of life was oppressive. I remember that Mother had told me that a man who worked for her father had been a soldier in India during the Mutiny and, when asked what he thought of the country, he had said that it was a land of wide dry fields and straight dusty interminable roads. That was his experience, but it fitted in well with what I saw on that first train journey. The Grand Trunk Road may appeal to the Romantics for its length across the Continent and for its wide undeviating course, often cutting fields in two, but to the traveller on foot it can be wearisome in the extreme. Only when the train approached Calcutta did the parched look give way to the rich green of Eastern India.

At Howrah station Staig met me with the news that I was to stay at the United Services Club. On the ship there had been a mystery man who, we heard, was a member of the Service which we had joined. He must have known why we were on the ship, but he had made no effort to speak to us, and it was hardly our place to approach him because, from his appearance, he seemed to be near retiring age. I never saw him in conversation with anybody, and every day he had the same deck chair in the same place on deck reading what could only be Homer in the original Greek. Someone who could read Greek, and only Greek, throughout a long voyage was daunting. He had been travelling on the same train to Calcutta, and was returning from leave to a posting in Bengal. And it was he who arranged that we stay at the Club, in the rooms on the ground floor usually reserved for casual visitors. We were given Honorary Temporary Membership of the Club. I never had an opportunity of thanking him for his help. He had gone back to his District before I arrived. When I mentioned his kindness to some members of the Club, I was told that his name was Blackwood and that he came from Scotland, but certainly not from Edinburgh. He was not too well liked, and took retirement shortly after the war ended.

Next day I acquired a bearer – probably the most essential acquisition for my existence in the country. He was a man from Orissa. He had most excellent 'chits', and had served a member of Finlays, the Managing Agents, who had some connection with Sir Ian Hamilton, one of the heroes of World War I. Bihar and Orissa had formed part of the Bengal Province until only a few years previously, and bearers from Orissa were widely employed, especially by the box-wallahs of Calcutta. They were reported to be unreliable at times and, after a few months' service, my man let me down when he failed to join me at the station in Lucknow to catch a train for Banur. When I was in Calcutta for a few days in 1945 that did not prevent him from coming to me seeking reinstatement. He seemed hardly a year older and just as glib. His pay seemed very small, but he explained that he would expect more as I rose in the Service. I had never had anybody to look after my clothes for me, brush my shoes, etc. and, at the time, was quite satisfied with his attentions.

Several of the High Officials were staying in the Club, and were most interested to hear of the voyage and the narrow escape from being torpedoed near Malta. Staig and I had to make formal calls on them in the Secretariat in Writers' Buildings, and we received instructions that the Governor would like to meet us. He was Lord Ronaldshay, son of the Marquis of Zetland, names which indicate the family's origins in the Orkneys of Scotland. He was one of a class of aristocrat that now seems obsolete, in that he had travelled extensively in countries of the Near and Middle East, and gained some experience of the ways and customs of the peoples of these lands, and had some sympathy with their beliefs and aspirations. It was only a very short interview, but it was encouraging.

Shopping

The well-stocked markets, and the amazing displays of fruit in the stalls, many of which were tropical and strange to me, would have impressed any newcomer from England at any time, but for someone who had just left the country and had endured rationing and restrictions it was breathtaking. I remember the dull meals at the Club in London where I had stayed, and the little variety that could be found in Edinburgh. I managed to find a store in Dharamsala prepared to send food parcels home, and the tins of butter and jam, especially the typaree (Cape gooseberry) jam, were most welcome.

There was also some serious shopping to be done. I think I went to Whiteaway Laidlaws – as being cheaper than Hall & Anderson and the Army & Navy – and invested in sheets, pillows, blankets, towels and a canvas bedding roll with straps on a cork mattress (the cork was in little packets which could be rolled up), and a tin wash hand basin with a leather cover and a handle so that it could be carried. I was assured that it was a necessity, as one never knew what nastiness lurked in the basins in the railway carriages. I did not find it a very useful purchase. And of course a MOSQUITO NET (I don't know how I forgot to mention that). Another useless purchase was a chill belt – a twelve-inch belt of knitted wool, to be worn in bed at nights to prevent chills on the stomach. I can't remember ever using it. I also had to get a topee – a workman-like one of Sola Pith, which was light and effective but ungainly. And, before I forget them, I ordered Visiting Cards at Thacker Spink – **Donald MacPherson, Indian Civil Service** – to be sent to my posting at Dacca in East Bengal. I was told that I should require them in a Station like Dacca, where there were numerous memsahibs, who expected any newcomer to call and, in order not to be disturbed, would hang a 'Not At Home' box on the garden gate. A card in a box equalled a formal call. It saved a newcomer hours of weariness. When one left a Station one would have to do the round again, marking the card with the letter PPC (*Pour Prendre Congée*). I may have spread my purchases over a second day but, with only 400 rupees, I could not indulge in an orgy of spending, and I had good advice to leave anything that was not too urgent till I got to Dacca, where a *durzee* would be able to run up something suitable. I did not have any time to see the sights of the town. I did not penetrate down Bow Bazaar or Dharamsala but, with the Maidan, the Victoria Memorial and the grounds of Government House, not to mention the series of Department Stores on Chowringhee, Calcutta belied its name of the

City of Dreadful Night. It had not lost the aura which it held before the transfer of the Capital of the Indian Empire to Delhi.

En route to Dacca

That second night I made arrangements for going to Dacca, having sent an advice to the Collector as soon as I had been informed of my posting. Though Christmas was so near, few were travelling to Dacca that night, so I had a first class compartment to myself. Possibly more were going to Calcutta for the festivities there. Anyway, I had ample space for my baggage, and the bearer rolled out my bedding on the lower berth and spread out the cork mattress and the sheets, blankets and pillow. The train left at 10 o'clock for the six to seven hour journey and, as soon as it was clear of Calcutta, I was glad of the blanket, as the air became very chilly. I had a good sleep, and was not too pleased to be wakened in the darkness to get down from the train and on to the river steamer.

When the railway was first laid, the terminus of the line on the bank of the Ganges had a station fit for a terminus until one night during the rainy season, when the river bank could no longer withstand the pressure of the strong current, and the station was washed away, and completely disappeared. The terminus is on the south bank of the Pabna, (as the Ganges is called at this point), opposite its junction with the Jamuna (as the Brahmaputra is called for most of its course in Bengal).

The train was standing in a sort of siding, which was very badly lit. There was no platform, so descent from the compartment required extreme caution, especially as the ground was muddy. Planks laid on mud provided the path to the river and the steamer. The planks were quite slippery and a bamboo railing gave only minimum support. After years of experience we became accustomed to such conditions in travel, and thought little of them, but to a newcomer who was barely awake and shivering from the cold breeze from the river, tackling the transfer from train to steamer in the dark was an unpleasant and almost hazardous adventure, not to be expected in a civilized country.

Compared with the train, the steamer had the comfort of a hotel. The bearer laid out my bedding etc. in a cabin, with washbasin etc. I went on to the forward deck for morning tea – never was tea so welcome – and watched the dawn growing lighter until the sun began to rise over the vast stretch of water. One began to see the fishing boats drawn up on the river bank, and the men preparing for the day's work – usually by clearing their throats!

Born and bred in a city, I had never seen a sunrise like this. The beauty of the awakening day as the light gathered strength and the sun shone over these wide rivers stirred in me a feeling of awe and wonder that was almost religious. It was a time for prayer, and had been so for millions since the distant past. Often, in the first decade of my service, when I was posted to Stations in East Bengal, I had to travel by the river steamers. When I was wakened, either for embarkation or disembarkation, I witnessed the beginning of a new day and never ceased to marvel at it. I was thrilled to the core by the experience and its significance. In West Bengal dawn was just something that happened once every twenty-four hours.

After tea I retired to my cabin to continue my broken sleep and recover from the very heavy curry tiffin which was served in the dining room. Narayanganj was reached about 1.30 and the SMO, Tim Graham, came and met me. The Collector, S.G. Hart, had deputed him to undertake this task. I was glad of his help in getting ashore. The railway station was much more established than at Goalando, and the train, being on the metre gauge, looked rather like a big toy in comparison with the trains on the standard gauge.

Dacca was only about ten or twelve miles away, but we did not reach it until after 3.00. We secured a tikka gharri to take us to the Collector's house in Ramna, which was the Official Quarter of the town. This part of the town had been developed when, for some ten

River steamer

63

years, Dacca had been the Capital of the Provinces of Eastern Bengal and Assam. The houses or bungalows were of a suitable standard for the influx of officials from the Secretariat and the many Departments required by a Government at its Capital. All the houses, therefore, were new and set in lovely gardens, and the roads were wide, tree-lined and well-kept, unlike the narrow streets of the Old Town near the railway station.

I was made most welcome by the Collector and his wife, and was given a very pleasant room and, with the SDO of Narayanganj, went down for tea in the garden, as one did in vicarage gardens and such-like places in the South of England. It was all very strange to me, and I must have seemed strange to the Collector and his wife, but they were most kind in overlooking my gaucherie. What did amaze me most of all was to see women smoking openly – they said it kept off the flies and mosquitoes – and drinking whisky. I knew some women at home did smoke cigarettes but always secretly and a trifle shamefacedly, but I never thought women touched whisky except for medicinal purposes. Men, of course, were different!

First posting: Dacca and impressions of the Courts

As the voyage had taken six weeks, I arrived in Dacca on either the 23rd or 24th of December, and for ten days the offices were closed during which time I was invited to parties, and enjoyed life. My first day of service was 2nd January 1918. In order to become acquainted with the work of the Courts I was detailed to sit with the Bengali Deputy Collector, who was SDO of the Headquarters Sub-Division of the Dacca District. I had seen some of the Courts at home, and was not prepared for the dirt and the casual manner in which business was conducted. The Court Room was large, and the white-washed walls were hanging with dirt and dust, while there were stains of betel juice near the floor. As it was January and therefore cold, according to the Deputy, the heavy louvred doors behind the dais on which we sat were closed against the breeze from the North. A railing round the dais kept the lawyers and the public at a distance. There seemed no sense of order or dignity. People came and went and chattered, and gave small heed to what was being said by the lawyers, the Deputy or the witnesses.

A great deal of time in the Criminal Courts of India, and in Bengal in particular, is taken up with Private Complaints. These are Private Prosecutions for small injuries, small mischiefs such as trespass on a neighbour's land and, because there had been a Christmas break, on the day the Courts opened for the New Year there was a very heavy backlog of complaints to be heard. The Peshkar, as the Magistrate's Clerk was called, sat alongside the Magistrate, took the first petition and told the peon or orderly to shout the name of the petitioner. A weedy-looking individual came along, followed by his Muktear (a subordinate who was less qualified and therefore a cheaper legal practitioner in the Court). He was guided to what took the place of the witness stand, and asked for his name and the relevant particulars.

The Muktear then asked him what he had to say, and he told his story. I did not understand what he was saying. I might have heard one or two words which I could recognise, but the language the witness was using differed vastly from the Bengali I had learned at the School of Oriental Studies in London. The East Bengal and Dacca dialects were not highly regarded by the pundits of Bengal, i.e. West Bengal and Calcutta, but this seemed to be another language and not a dialect. The Magistrate explained the draft of the man's statement to me, which he recorded in English for the Record. After the Magistrate had asked the complainant or petitioner a few questions to satisfy himself that there was prima facie evidence that some injury had been done, he ordered a Summons to be issued for the person accused to attend Court in about a fortnight's time. This complainant stood down, and another was called, and so it went on for nearly two hours. In one or two instances, when the alleged offence seemed very petty, he sent the papers to a local Worthy of repute and reliability for a report before deciding whether a Summons was to be issued.

Then an old woman was called. She was almost skin and bone, but full of anger and so eager to talk that she would not wait for the formalities of her name, place of abode and the name of the person she was accusing to be recorded. It was her son-in-law. Her Muktear gave her what help he could to secure coherence in her accusation. He asked her to speak up, for she would keep her face covered so that the crowd in the court could not see any of her features. The Magistrate asked her to speak up, but she hid her face even closer. At length the Muktear and the Magistrate managed to discover what had brought her to Court. She and the son-in-law had had words, and what she said had so annoyed him that he had hit her across the back towards the rump with a cane. I did hear the word *mara* repeated and repeated, and there were *dags* – that is marks and bruises.

She had heard that, in order to establish the truth of any allegation of assault, the marks should be shown to the Court so, covering her face with her sari more closely than before, she lifted her cloth higher and higher, so that practically everything that is generally hidden was exposed. The Muktear was quite worried. 'Ma, Ma,' he said, 'that is quite sufficient,' but Ma would not listen. She raised the cloth even higher and turned round and round in the witness stand to ensure that the marks had been noticed, all the while muttering, '*Dags, dags,*' and keeping her sari over her face. I did not see any marks, and I think the Magistrate took them on trust for he ordered a Summons to be issued on the son-in-law, in the hope that the pair of them would have made up their differences before the real day of hearing. I had the impression that she was a cantankerous old woman – but she may have had a grievance. I stayed to hear two or three more complaints, and then left the Court. What amazed me was the indifference of everyone in the Courtroom to the behaviour of the old woman. It was something that could not happen in the formal atmosphere of a Court in England and, as far as I know, the Dacca press never reported the incident.

That was my first experience of a Court in Bengal, and it was typical of many in which I was to officiate. It was probably dirtier than most and, even after I had gained a greater facility with Bengali, I found listening to evidence in that vernacular for any length of time, and mentally translating it into English for writing up the record or substance of what had been said, very exhausting. So I shall not pursue this subject any further now.

1918: Army Days
Well, for only just under twelve months I was a Lieutenant in the IARO (Indian Army Reserve of Officers) and during that brief period I travelled more across India and saw more of the country than in all my civilian days until Independence. At the time I felt frustrated, but now I am glad that I had the experience and the chance of seeing the North West Frontier at first hand – the scene of war and vigilance and of the romantic fiction of the day. It was a hostile land which still held a great fascination, and was so different from the flat green plains of Bengal.

There was a Volunteer Corps in Dacca, with a Major promoted from Sergeant in charge, which I joined, as was expected, a few weeks after my arrival. I don't remember much about the duties that were to be performed, but I do know that on two occasions I did not receive the orders to guard some place or other until hours after I was supposed to report for duty. The Major was annoyed, but realised that I was not at fault. He said he would see that I got the orders, the next time they were issued, but there was no next time, as by then I had received my Commission and orders to proceed to Peshawar. After I had been less than nine months in Dacca the Government of India had suggested that I should have a Medical Examination and, if passed as fit, undertake military duties. The Civil Surgeon gave me a thorough overhaul, and was satisfied until he took out a stamp and asked me its colour. I could see it was either a 1 anna or a half anna stamp (one being red and the other green) but could not be certain of its value. I guessed red – it was green – and the Civil Surgeon wrote against the Medical Report in very bold letters 'COLOUR BLIND' which was the reason I was to attend nothing more martial than a Sanitary Course.

En route to Peshawar I pre-gathered at the US (United Services) Club with Staig, who had travelled out with me on the *Sardinia*, and collected such necessary equipment as had been presented, and the uniform. We were advised to go to the Regimental Tailor at Fort William. He took our measurements one day, and had everything ready for us the following afternoon. Not until twenty years later, or more, did we hear of the marvellous Chinese in Hong Kong etc. who could turn out a made-to-measure suit in a matter of twenty-four hours. Of course the material was only khaki drill, which may be easier to work with than tweed or worsted, and much less expensive, but the cut was good. I must confess that when I found myself in shorts I felt only half dressed, but that feeling went after a very few hours. I also sat for a photo in uniform (postcard size) for sending to the family at home, and some other friends.

The month was May and hot. Trains were not filled up with all the modern contrivances to moderate the temperature, not even electric fans, so Staig and I had an ice-box, or rather a box with ice which, as it melted, would cool the air. This was, I believe, quite customary but I did not think it did much to ameliorate the discomfort of rail travel at such times, and I never had another one.

After a night in the train we reached Lahore about mid-day, just missing the expected connection. We had time after lunch to take a tonga (an open two-wheeled conveyance) for a short tour of the town, but in the heat the streets were deserted and depressing, and we were glad to spend the hours before the next connecting train arrived in the station waiting room. There was another night in the train, and many sweltering hours during the day had to be endured before we reached Peshawar in the afternoon.

We had been told that hotels for Military Officers did not exist, and none was advertised in the newspapers we had picked up en route, so we had to go to the Dak Bungalow – a large solid structure with little accommodation, in spite of its size. It must have been built about the time of the Mutiny, when safety rather than comfort was the most important requirement. Consequently, the rooms had an airlessness which was almost unbearable when the temperature rose above 100 degrees. I remember Staig and I each had two if not three cold baths (tin tubs of course) during the afternoon and evening. We were the only occupants at the time and, when looking at the Register for calculating what was due for our stay, I noticed that the number of visitors was low, and had declined steadily over the years. At one time, however, most of the great men of the Indian Army had stayed there and left their signatures in the Visitors' Book, which thus became a record of more than ephemeral interest. The list included 'Bob' – Lord Roberts – of the March from Kabul to Kandahar which, before 1914, was an epic achievement.

The food was no better and no worse than typical Dak Bungalow fare, and it was with great relief that we heard we could have quarters in the RAMC Mess. The rooms were spacious and opened on to a garden where fig trees were growing, and the officers did not indulge in medical shoptalk at the table, and made us feel that we were not outsiders. Another ICS man joined us for the Sanitary Course – Philpot, with whom I had a close connection during my years in Settlement. He was one of the shyest and most silent men I have ever known – thin and tall and saddled with as unwieldy a mouthful of forenames as might be imagined: Hamlet (bad enough to start with) Cunningham Vachell!

The course was not strenuous. I have forgotten practically everything, but we had to be in attendance by 6.00 a.m. or as near that hour as possible, and we were finished for the day by 11.30. After that hour it was too hot to concentrate. I do remember lectures on avoiding cholera in an epidemic without recourse to an injection and to the construction of an incinerator, which would be effective in the dry hot climate of Northern India but useless in the humidity of Bengal. We also visited the centre for pasteurising milk for the protection of the supplies to the town, though it was discovered afterwards that the RAMC doctors were not as careful or cautious as they were expected to be about supervising the treatment of the milk that came to the Mess.

Staig had hammer toes, and was unable to go on long walks so, for exercise of an evening, Philpot and I went exploring the outskirts of the cantonment. There was not much to see for, although the mountains rose only a short distance away, the land round Peshawar was as flat as the proverbial pancake, and the roads were very dusty. We avoided the old town. One evening I went there alone and, when I returned, was informed that I should not have gone there towards sunset. I might have lost my way when darkness fell, and that would have been very dangerous. I did try to keep up a conversation with Philpot as we went along, but with his long legs, one step of his equalled two of mine, and I was often out of breath and talking was like a series of gasps.

The Mess must have been situated close to the Cantonment Cemetery. Every day before sunset, I could hear the Funeral March and the Last Post. Some poor soul had succumbed to the heat and life in the Indian Barracks. Many of them were casualties of the War – just as much as those in France. They were men passed fit for service abroad (not active service because of their age or physical condition) and they were unable to stand a heat to which they were unaccustomed or to adjust their habits to the Indian conditions.

As part of the Course, we were sent for a fortnight to Cherah, a small hill station near Rawalpindi for Military Personnel and Military Personnel only, so that they could have short breaks from the prolonged intense heat during the hot weather. There was no Club and I cannot recollect any bazaar. The hills on which it was perched were bleak, barren and rocky, like the hills we had seen rising from the Eastern shores of the Red Sea. There was only one postcard obtainable. It merely showed a small cluster of buildings sited awkwardly on a hillside, and was printed in Germany – and this was during the War! I cannot remember the Mess to which we were attached for the fortnight of our stay. but it was most friendly and the evenings passed very quickly.

During one course we saw an inspection line-up – not the inspection however, which seemed little more than in and out. We also saw how a Canteen was managed and given the beer for the troops to taste. It was Murree Beer, brewed in a small cantonment in the Hills for the troops, and I believe for the troops only. This was my first taste of beer – aged twenty four – which just shows how many changes there have been since 1918!

On returning to Pershawar we had only a few weeks of our course left. and I caught sandfly fever. The sandfly is so small that the mosquito net does not keep it out. It is not a serious fever but most annoying and makes one prone to prolonged sleepiness throughout the day.

Before the end, however, I took time off for a visit to the Khyber. I thought, and thought rightly, that I might not be in Peshawar again, and was determined to see it. I got the required permit, hired a tonga and set off. For the first twelve miles or so the road is absolutely level, then the narrow pass rises abruptly, and I saw the lookout posts high up on the rocks amid mementoes of the Regiments that had passed along this route. I did not go the whole way, but stopped where there was some water and what I think was a mosque. It was so very peaceful, for there was no traffic through the pass. I never met any cart or any men from the Hills. It was late afternoon when I returned to Preshawar, and I remember how the humid heat struck me as we left the pass and reached the plain. There is a complete system of irrigation for the gardens of the cantonment, and I could feel the warm damp air rising up my trousers. The driver, in spite of a tough dry skin, wrapped the end of his turban round his face so that only his eyes were visible, and I could feel the glass of my spectacles getting hotter and hotter and becoming uncomfortable to my eyes. The temperature that day according to the meteorological reports was 131 degrees in the shade!

I had received no posting when the course ended and, after consultation, had no alternative but to return to Dacca. That journey back was without missed connections, which I had come to accept as inevitable. The trains were all on time. I broke my journey at Benares to stay with Desai, one of the Indians who had been recruited to the ICS in London after the Examinations. I had seen more of him in London than of the others, and he had accompanied me at Aden, when we went to see 'Solomon's Tanks'. He had been posted to the United Provinces, and had offered to show me round Benares. He was a most excellent host.

He took me through the narrow streets, little more than alleyways really, and we visited the Sculpted Temples, with most explicit carvings. He also arranged for me to call on the Maharajah, one of the old Royal Families, but, as the front was in the process of being repaired, we entered by a back stair. To my amazement, there were lots of dhotis drying from the palace windows – even if it were only the back. The Maharajah was in a long salon, which was empty except for the tawdriest pictures in the European manner on the walls. I have seen such salons in the Palaces of the Rajahs of Bengal, but never such an exhibition of tastelessness. He ought to have had some better guidance.

He did not have much to say for himself and suggested that we see his treasures in his Armoury. This was an amazing collection of priceless jewelled weapons.

We travelled by police launch down the Ganges at dawn, when the bathers were having their first ceremonial immersion, and the fires in the funeral pyres had not been lit. I went by myself to Sarnati, one of the sacred places of Buddhism, which was only a few miles away. I'm glad I saw Benares under his guidance. We corresponded for some three years or more – and then blank. I wrote and heard nothing. His name was not in the Civil List for the UP, and I suppose he had died.

Lucknow

I had had about a week in Benares, not long enough to get into harness again, when I received a posting to Labour Corps in Allahabad. I was acquainted with the Principal of the College there and knew he would show me around. However, an Officer was waiting for me when the train reached Allahabad Station to say that the posting was changed, and I was to carry on to Lucknow and, with that, he handed me the Railway Warrant for the unexpected addition to my journey. It was late when I reached Lucknow and everything was in darkness. I went to the only hotel I had heard of there. It was a ramshackle place. The dinner was poor and after the meal, when I was sitting on the veranda, the only other resident, an elderly member of the Police, asked me what I was doing there. He then proceeded to tell me some rather surprising things about the place, which made me wish my stay there would be brief.

Next morning, when I presented myself at the Depot, my arrival came as a surprise, but the unexpected seemed quite normal. There was little for me to do to begin with, and I was introduced to the Indian Warrant Officers, both Sikhs. The Subadar Major, a grey-haired stalwart with a mesh on his beard, had been with Roberts on the Kabul to Kandahar Marsh, and had justly earned the respect and trust of everyone. The Jamadar Sahib was capable but lacked the other's authority. The men of the Corps had been recruited from the villages, and were an extraordinary crowd. Many of them had never before left their villages, and were overwhelmed with the bustle all round them. They were quite unused to the uniforms which had been supplied. One man displayed himself wearing one puttee – but not on a leg. He had twisted it round his loins in as discreet a manner as could be imagined, yet never seemed to feel it scratchy. And there was another,

71

himself just a coolie like the others, who could command obedience from them. He claimed to be of the old Imperial Family of Delhi, and said he drew a pension from the British Government of India under the arrangements made after the Mutiny. When the Emperor was deprived of all power and authority all the members of his family drew pensions also, but the shares must have been very small because the number of descendants of the Emperor had increased out of reckoning. He did not restrict himself to one wife and had very many sons. One could not doubt his word. He had one eye and, to look at him in profile with his good eye, was to see the face of Aurangzeb, as depicted by the painters of the Mogul Court. For me, communication with these men was limited at that time. They did not understand Bengali, of which I knew a little, and such Hindustani as I had learned was only partially intelligible to them. Though I did not give any real assistance in bringing some sort of order to these bewildered villagers, in the course of about ten days order did emerge, and the Corps was ready when orders came that it was to proceed to the Frontier to Banur in Baluchi Territory.

During that period of transformation I was staying at a sort of Chummery, which was run by the Officer of the Depot (I never knew his rank or even if he had one) and his wife. They had one of these rambling old-fashioned bungalows with rooms opening off one or perhaps two large central rooms. When he heard I was staying at Clark's he said I had better come along to his place, where I would meet more congenial company, and I was very glad to accept. I think there were three other officers besides myself, and I have forgotten two of them completely. One, who was a Major, was the embodiment of the caricature of a 'Poonah Officer'. I never thought they existed until I met him. He was an authority on everything, and never ceased to put himself forward. He talked a great deal, but what I remember most, because it aggravated me so much, was that he had a fund of what he thought was wit. He insisted on explaining the point he wanted to make with a little wheeze in his voice, especially when the point was a trifle risqué or salacious. Still, listening to him was preferable to sitting alone in the dark in Clark's Hotel. For the fortnight I was there, Lucknow was without electricity. The petrol lamps had to be brought back and, although they did give some light, they generated heat. Since it was August, it was at its hottest and most intolerable. What was worse was that the electric fans were tantalizingly motionless. All the old pull punkas had been taken down and cast away when the electricity

72

came to the town. For everybody that fortnight was a very exhausting time.

I did, however, manage to see some of the sights. There was the Residency – roofless, and with the walls scarred by cannon shot. The old Sikh veteran who acted as guide and recounted the story of the siege in great detail was most derisive of the officers of the time. The Sahibs of today were not a patch on the Sahibs he knew when he was a lad and joined the Army. I saw the La Martinière School founded by a Frenchman attached to the old Court of Oudh and which, I was proudly told, had provided the model for the White City in Earl's Court or Shepherd's Bush. On a postcard it seemed to rival the Taj in beauty. In reality it looked like something in a fairground, almost derelict.

On the last day of the fortnight (it was a Saturday) the power was restored, and everyone in the chummery went to the cinema. There would be no such pleasures in Banur.

Banur

The troop-train left on the Sunday evening. I did not accompany the men to the station. The Subadar Major and the Jamadar saw to that, but everything was satisfactorily arranged, and there were no absentees. My bearer, however, never arrived. He knew that the corps was to go to the tribal area, where life for him would have been unbearable, yet he never said anything to me. Had he done so, I should have understood, and engaged a Lucknow Muslim. He had been given money that morning to purchase some material for a turban he needed, and he had promised to be at the station in good time before the train left but he never arrived. He was Hindu servant class from Orissa, and afterwards I was told they were often untrustworthy. I was to see him again in Calcutta twenty seven years afterwards. In appearance he had not altered much. He did not look much older, except that grey hairs were showing among the black, and he was as spare as I had known him. I was staying for a day or so at the US (United Services) Club and, as servants were a problem in 1945, we should have been glad of an efficient man. He presented himself and brushed aside any reference to his lapse at Lucknow. He could not appreciate that there had been a dereliction of duty, and always remembered that I had been a kind, considerate and generous master. I was not to be taken in a second time. I must have been a fool in 1918.

The train was no express. It trundled its way through the night and into the following day, stopping for long periods between stations. It was nearing noon before it reached Lahore, where it was shunted into a siding as far as possible from the main station, so that a halt could be made to feed the troops. The time allowed was generous – too generous it seemed because, when the train moved on, it stopped for about ten minutes to give the CO and me a chance to have a bite, and I was nearly left behind as it started again when I was paying the bill. The communication cord had to be pulled.

The train continued its slow halting progress through the hot dusty afternoon, and at Rawalpindi turned southward along the eastern bank of the Indus to Mari Indus, where there was a steam ferry for the crossing of the river. When we arrived at the other side, we had to entrain again for the last leg of the journey to Banur. The carriages were small, and more uncomfortable than the carriages of the main line, and with fewer amenities to moderate the daytime heat. It was uncomfortable enough for Lyall and myself, but the men were packed like sardines in these box-like compartments, and must have been exhausted. There was a report that, on a recent journey when the troops carried were Gurkhas, two died from heat stroke in the trains. Coming from the cooler hills, they could not stand up to these high temperatures in such stuffy compartments.

Two days were spent in Banur for final preparations. Lyall and I were at the Officers' Mess, which was very pleasant. In August Banur was at its dullest. Women are sent to the hills with the onset of the hot weather and, as a result, it had the appearance of a very ghostly orthodox Moslem town, where no female is to be seen. It was very dusty. The shops were small, and many of the houses had those thick mud walls which kept out the fiercest heat.

As a preliminary to the final stage of the journey, a march to Khajuri, a move was made to a camping site on the outskirts of the town, as close to the boundary of British India as was practicable. The reason for this was that the road, the upgrading of which was to be the work of this Labour Corps, lay in Tribal Territory, and was open for traffic, including the movement of troops and auxiliaries, until noon, and not a minute later. To ensure that the destination could be reached before 12 o'clock, the march had to begin as soon as the road was open. I think this was 6.00 a.m. No tents were pitched. Everyone slept in the open, and I remember it as a brilliant starlit night. The timetable that had been set was rigidly adhered to, and the Corps was on the road as soon as it was open to traffic. Fortunately there was no incident on the march but the men, accustomed to walking barefoot across fields, found

74

stiff army boots and puttees a sore trial. As I had to accompany them, I had to wear uniform and that included boots (fortunately not army boots) and puttees, so I could sympathise with them. A good few of the men limped into camp at the final destination. I forget now what was the distance that had to be travelled. I have an idea it was some fifteen to seventeen miles. It may even have been twenty. Nobody could gainsay that it was a very long slog in tiring conditions on a very hot day. For a good part of the way the road, which followed the course of the Tochi river, lay at the foot of steep rocky slopes but, as it neared Khajuri, the valley opened out, and the fort stood at the beginning of a fairly long stretch of level ground well above the level of the river. The only other prominent feature of the site was a very old date palm, the only tree that could be seen for miles and miles along the road, but one that could provide no shade to a weary traveller. It was so conspicuous in that barren land that it had given its name to the fish (*khajur gach* is the Bengali and the general Indian name for the date palm). It yielded no fruit and was not topped for the making of toddy, the naturally fermented juice or sap of the date palm. There were about eight men of the Frontier or Tribal Auxiliaries stationed in the Fort. I never saw them on the road, but they were inspected at infrequent intervals.

The Camp was spacious but fenced and, in addition to the accommodation for the men, there were tents for Lyall and myself, for an Indian doctor and for an Officer of the Military Works Department, MacRosty by name. There was also an office tent. All the tents, however, were only single ply and gave little protection from the heat

The Camp

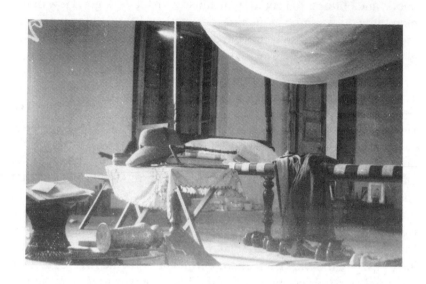

My billet

Blasting on the roads

of August, when the official temperature rose as high as 120 degrees in the shade, and there was no shade. Also, we had no servants and had selected one or two of the coolies to do what was needed and, however willing they might have been, they were very rough and unused to the ways of sahibs. The most trying was the one who prepared our meals. He knew only two soups – soup Yorkshire relish and soup Worcester sauce – which we got on alternate days and only two puddings – baked custard and bread fried in a sort of syrup. Meat was either goat or chicken. Since those days of Khajuri I have had a prejudice against Yorkshire relish, Worcester sauce and baked custard!

The day after arriving the men seemed none the worse for their long march and, armed with spades and pickaxes, were out on the road. They carried large stones for the soling of the road and bound them with soil which they had dug. My task was to see that they did a good job, and did not slack. For protection when I went on the road I had two mounted guards. They both carried guns and came from one of the neighbouring villages that were just visible from the Camp. They were called *badrigas* (I am uncertain of the correct spelling), and their employment as guards was in line with the plans for bringing peace in this tribal territory. They looked fierce, but I found them helpful and considerate. On one occasion when, after a bout of malaria, I had gone to inspect the progress of the roadwork, they thought I would

My own special badriga

find the steep short incline from the river to the Camp too tiring after spending hours in the hot sun, and they insisted that I mount one of their horses. The saddle was of a type that I had never seen, and not very comfortable, but I was glad that I did not have to trudge up even that short hill, and I did appreciate their kindness.

I had been little more than a fortnight at Khajuri when I had my first attack of malaria, which I had caught through being foolhardy and sleeping in the open at night without a mosquito net. At least that is what I was told but now, looking back and with more experience of the fever, I believe it was in Banur that the mosquito made me its victim. At Khajuri there was none of the stagnant water the mosquitoes love, and I cannot remember seeing one during all the months I was at the Camp. The continuing high temperatures reaching 120 degrees made rest in the afternoon and even at night quite intolerable. The tents were only single ply and never intended for use in such conditions. There was little relief from the heat at night: only a few degrees. The sleeper under a mosquito net could have no benefit from it; he would feel suffocated and breathless, a prisoner in a hot airless cell, from which only sunrise could bring respite. I was so worn out by these restless nights that I had every excuse for having my bed removed to the open air outside the net.

The Doctor was a Madrassi and I believe had a commission in one of the Medical Services, though I never knew what his rank was. But I could not think of him as being of the IMS (Indian Medical Service) which usually consisted of men of a different calibre altogether. One feature which surprised me in a doctor was that he had two holes in the lobes of his ears. They were quite large, and must have been required for some adornment. Somehow it did not inspire confidence in his ability. He took my temperature, diagnosed malaria and mentioned quinine. Now from 1914 a concoction called ammoniated tincture of quinine was the staple remedy for flu or a very bad cold, and a vile nasty-tasting mixture it was. Once I remember having had more than I liked of the nauseous stuff, and I had temporary deafness or partial deafness. I told the doctor I did not want quinine, and told him the reason. He seemed to accept that I would not take quinine, but he gave me nothing in its place, not even something to reduce the temperature as was customary in the thirties, if malaria had not been established by blood tests. So the temperature remained high but what was worse was that I could not take any food. I could only take tea – without toast – and lemon squash. On the fourth day the doctor said I had to have an intramuscular injection. He gave it to me on my right arm instead of on my posterior, as I had hoped, and I had intermittent pain in that arm for the better part of a year. Whatever the cause, whether he gave me too weak an injection or not, the fever continued unabated. On the fifth day the ADMS (Assistant Director of Medical Services) visited the Camp en route for Miranshah at the end of the Tochi Road, and promised to look in again the next day on his return to Banur. He added that he thought I should leave to go to hospital. The next day I remember trying to shave properly to show that I ought not to be sent to hospital, but my efforts seemed to prove how ill I was, and the ADMS said an ambulance would be sent the next day, as it was too late to get one from Banur before the road closed at noon.

After his departure I had a bath (there was not much water to spare at the Camp for too many of such luxuries), but I could not get out of the tin tub until MacRosty came and helped me up. The ambulance was late the next day, and I had a bumpy ride back to Banur to be off the road by midday. The hospital seemed so very civilized but, because it was August and hot weather, there were no nice nurses, only medical orderlies who were equally efficient. There was no doubt of the treatment – quinine (liquid quinine it was too) three times a day in 15 gram doses. On my first leave in Dublin Street, when I asked for a 5 gram tablet, he had never heard of such a strong dose. The taste of quinine, and it is not pleasant but lasting, was never out of my mouth from breakfast to bedtime. I had strict instructions not to attempt to leave my bed. After my first attempt to reach the *ghusul khana* (bathroom) I collapsed on the floor. This drastic treatment, however, was effective. The fever left me and I felt able to eat something more substantial than tea and lemon squash and, after the fare at Khajuri, the food seemed splendid. I recovered very rapidly. There was a very good library in the hospital, and the standard of the books was high, in spite of most of them being light literature.

Lyall had to be in hospital for two days and, when he was there, the General came to see how we were. The Labour Corps had not been a month at Khajuri and, when he had been to inspect it the previous day, he found both the British Officers absent in hospital! He was rather a hero in those days as he was a pioneer in the Everest Expeditions. After about four days I was allowed to rise, though I still spent a good many of the daytime hours dozing in bed. At the end of the week I was considered fit enough to go back to Camp if I wanted and, when MacRosty who had come to Banur on Military Works affairs called to see how I was, he agreed to take me back in his side-car. That was the first and only time I have been in a side-car, and it was certainly a very bumpy ride.

By this time the fierce heat which we had to endure on our arrival had gone and the weather, though hot, was dry and just bearable. The men seemed to be working harder than they had done before my fever, and I was pleasantly surprised at the progress of the road. Inspection became a routine, though effective, duty, but there was much to interest one in the nature of the country and the travellers from the Tribal Hinterland, Afghanistan and Baluchistan. The clear air made photography a joy; every snap almost guaranteed a picture which one could exhibit with satisfaction if not pride, and there was none of the worry I had experienced in Bengal over deciding on the correct exposure. Unfortunately all the films had to be sent in to Banur for development and some of the best rolls did not return, though prints from them had been seen in the photographers. However I was more than satisfied with the prints that I did receive. None of these men from the hills raised any objection to my taking photos of them. They would laugh, say 'Stang Marsh', or something like that, and I might be offered a bit of chapatti by a grimy hand. It was no delicacy, but to refuse would have been insulting and a rejection of friendliness. I knew no Pushti, the language of these hills, and my Hindustani was less than fluent. I could only smile my thanks.

Shortly after I returned from hospital Lyall received orders to take command of a corps (Labour Corps) in Persia. He did suggest to the powers that be that I might also go there with him which I should have welcomed, in the hope that I might see Persepolis and other relics of Cyrus; but the destination was Bandarabas where temperatures equalled those that had been experienced on our arrival, and the countryside was barren and featureless. He was told that, on account of my fever, it would be an unsuitable place for me. I was sorry to lose him as a CO and we kept up a correspondence for a good many years until we were both married.

His successor, a District Engineer, was an entirely different person. The District Engineers had not the prestige or qualifications of a member of the Public Works Department, and I have an idea he had done part of his training in India. His chief object, after coming to Khajuri, was to be transferred back to India and the United Provinces District of Bareilly, if not permanently, at any rate to enjoy some leave. I was told he had been instructed to inform headquarters if I had any more attacks of fever.

Until the cold weather arrived I had a recurrence of malaria about once a fortnight, each time less severe, but no report was sent because Sinclair knew that, if I were to go, his chances of having leave to visit India again would be nil. I did not know at the time that Headquarters had been worried about my fever, and I was pleased to be staying on because, as the days grew chillier, I felt rejuvenated and able to cope with the dreariness of the time spent in Camp.

I had nothing in common with Sinclair. We had no mutual interests nor did we have the same sense of humour. I did not like him in a passive sort of way. We never had a quarrel but, to get control of my nerves on several occasions, I found perfectly sound reasons in connection with the work of the Corps for spending the night away from the Camp in the inspection rest rooms in two of the forts along the road: Saidgi, which was near Banur, perched on the rocky hillside, and Ldak nearer Miranshah, which was on a wide stretch of the River Tochi, where walnut trees line its bank. It was such a relief to be free of his presence for a night or two, despite the absence of anything to read except for copies of the *Tatler* & *Bystander* of several years before 1914. I could hardly believe there had been such changes in so short a time, as these old magazines showed. The humour seemed terribly unfunny. Perhaps my unease was heightened because, for some months after leaving Peshawar, I had no mail from home and, especially when in bed with fever, I worried at the absence of news from home, fearing it could only be bad. The first of the flu epidemics at the close of the War had just begun at home, and was taking its toll of life. When it did at last come, the mail was worth waiting for, and by then I had been freed from the recurrence of the malaria.

One matter I must mention: on three consecutive days in the middle of September I received a payslip for my August salary from three different DDOs (Divisional Disbursing Officer). I never met such generosity from the Army again. I had to wait a very long time for my pay on my return to the Civil Service – and there was only one of these pays that I could accept.

By Treaty the presence of personnel of the Indian Armed Forces was limited to the road from Banur to Miranshah and then only until noon. The villages which could be seen from the road were out of bounds, but an opportunity to visit them came when the Government of India had arranged for a Survey of the incidence of malaria amongst the people of the Tochi valley. An invitation was given that our presence

81

would be welcomed. It would have been churlish to refuse. Guides and horses were to be provided. I was to see many similar villages during the course of my service and handle many social or welfare enquiries into village conditions and amenities but this, my first visit, made the most lasting impression.

This was not only because of its novelty for me, but also because our guides came from the villages and could only lead us to their own villages and no further, on account of a blood feud with the men of a neighbouring village. This feud would have had to be honoured in spite of the presence of privileged outsiders on a goodwill mission under the auspices of the Government of India. So, after the examination of his children had been completed, the man who led us to the first village only took us as far as a fixed point on the boundary of that village where he left us. We waited there until a guide came from the second village after being assured that the other man had departed and was not likely to return.

We may have visited three villages. I can only recollect two, the second being by far the more important. The thick mud walls that seemed to surround the village were in fact the walls of the houses in the village, which were so close together. They were without doors – for protection. The village roads were narrow and winding. The headman's house, where the investigation was to take place, surprised us by its size. The courtyard round which the houses of the various members of his family were ranged was large enough to contain not only the party of Medical Officers, but also his guests and all the male

Fisher giving out coins to the examined children

82

inhabitants of the village. The courtyards had been swept clean, and the IMS Major sat on a charpoy, with a bright carpet for covering. I was on a charpoy at the side, which had been placed on all the sweepings of the courtyard. The object of the investigation was to ascertain a) the incidence of malaria amongst the young and b) the effects of the recent influenza epidemic. The number of deaths had been unexpectedly high. These men of the Tribes appeared so strong and so hardy that one would have thought them capable of resisting any epidemic. The incidence of malaria was determined by the number of enlarged spleens found amongst the children, who were ranged up before the IMS Major. They were told to raise their loose shirts while he felt for their spleens. They were rewarded with a few annas of baksheesh for their trouble. More than 50 per cent of the children seemed to have had enlarged spleens, which meant a very high incidence of malaria.

To finish, there was what might be called a 'curry lunch' – no plates or knives and forks. The curry was poured into chapattis, formed into cone-shaped cups. It was good hot stuff and we broke off bits of chapatti, and dipped them in the mixture, and fished for chunks of lamb or possibly goat. It was a vastly different curry from what the cooks had served at table and, of course, we could lick our fingers clean. Bowls of water and a towel were also passed round.

This was probably the most interesting day of my entire military career. I took a number of photographs which are a vivid reminder of this most memorable day. Enlargements of one or two of them were taken for the official report.

I was surprised to learn how heavy the toll of the flu epidemic had been in the villages of the valley because, amongst the men of the Labour Corps, not one man went down with it. I had given strict orders that no one should have any contact with outsiders, and I think these orders were followed, not so much because they were my orders but more because the coolies from the United Provinces were afraid of the 'Wild Men of the Hills'. Our only loss was the old Subadar Major, who had served with 'Bob'. He came to me and said that he had heard of a death amongst his family at home and needed to go home to console and, if possible, help those who remained. He never came back. He too caught the fatal flu.

One other occasion stands out in my memory from the dull routine of those days. The Staff at the Ldak Fort had a celebration for the Armistice. A triumphal arch of bamboos and coloured paper had been erected. There was dancing and refreshments (Indian style), but no alcohol for this was Moslem territory. The Fort was the largest in the valley, and the courtyard was quite spacious. To Western eyes all-male dancing seemed very strange, and many of the dances were little more than 'Ring-a-Ring-a-Roses' with grown men instead of children, to a throbbing drum accompaniment. Very tedious they appeared to me. But the Sword Dance, a solo by a greybeard with arcs of iron for the sword and nerves of iron for the spectators, was as spectacular as some dervish-type dances. With the speed at which the dancers swirled round and round, their wide shirts spread out almost horizontally. I was glad to have attended the Armistice celebrations because 11th November had been a blank day at the Camp. The news only came through to us on the 14th, by which time the first excitement and exaltation were over. We did not even feel the desire to drink to the end of the war at last, and Sinclair only talked of the improvement of his chances of an early return home via Bareilly.

That day at Ldak seemed to inaugurate a long era of peace, but for months a hostile force from across the Border attacked the Fort. MacRosty happened to be there at the time. He was killed. I never learnt the circumstances. The reporting was very sketchy. He had helped me and I was grateful. He was hoping for his demob. so that he could return to England and marry the girl who was waiting for him.

The two veterans of the sword dance at Ldak

By this time it was the end of November, and one could hear the birds which had returned for the cold weather. The days might be bright and sunny, but the nights made one long for a big roaring fire. The single ply tents, which had been no protection against the fierce heat, were equally unable to provide warmth when it would have been most welcome.

There was always a thin sheet of ice on the water in the Camp washbasin, and I would go out with my overcoat and jacket (it was khaki drill) and cardigan (also khaki) which I would discard one after the other as the day got warmer until I was going around in my shirt sleeves. The *badriga* took charge of them for me.

By this time real progress on the road could be seen. The men were working together in a more disciplined way, and in the colder weather were working harder. Their hours were shorter too, because they could not leave the Camp as early as they did in the hot weather, but they still had to be off the road by 12.00. The bridge over the Tochi was now beginning to look like a bridge – a very long bridge – because the river which, for most of the year, was little more than a ditch, could rise dangerously after heavy rain. Yet, as the valley was wide, the flood spread out and was not very deep.

It was great weather for photography, and the people coming from the hills with their children and their donkeys, on their way to seek work or to beg in India (now Pakistan), made most effective pictures. The films had to be sent to Banur for developing, and some were returned. What gratified me was that some of the snaps I took of the Medical Malaria Inspection, after enlargement, were used for the Report of the Government of India.

Christmas, when it came, was merely just one dull day like all the other dull days of the previous four months. The Camp coolie/cook could not have coped with a regular Christmas feast had he been asked, so Sinclair and I sat down to two almost silent meals of the regular Worcester Sauce soup, goat and baked custard The Christmas mail had been held up somewhere along the line, so there was little for either of us to feel cheerful about. There was, of course, no work done that day, but there was no place to which we could go. Nonetheless, one could not help feeling the exhilaration of being amongst those old barren rocky hills, hills of history, danger and adventure.

On Christmas Eve, before retiring, I had gone outside to look across the valley. There was absolute silence, and the sharp outline of the mountains and the nearer heights were as visible in the clear cold moonlight as they were during the day. I could not help being reminded of the pictures of the Holy Land in the Bibles at home, and inevitably of the shepherds watching their flocks by night. I wonder if such thoughts would have occurred to me if I had come to the place fresh from a University today.

I missed the friendliness which had welcomed me to Dacca the previous year, as also the seven days' vacation between Christmas and the New Year, the civil celebrations of the 'Burra Din' (Big Day) and it was back to the road on what would have been Boxing Day. However, the Indian NCOs (Subadar and Jamadar) had their own party at the Fort, to which we were invited. It was a very dull dark place for a party which we then found was very formal in a way. We had the usual Indian sweets, then were offered whisky which we had to accept. We had small half pegs topped up in the glass with soda. The Indian ICS had tumblerfuls of the spirit with about a dessertspoonful of soda water to show they knew the custom. What iron insides these Sikhs must have had! It was a sort of end of the year party and unintentionally prophetic. Within a day or so I received orders to go to Miranshah, and Sinclair had his wish to return to Bareilly. His relief was a planter: a man used to dealing with coolies in his work, and thoroughly trustworthy. I could have worked very well with him but, after Khajuri, Miranshah was luxury.

I was to stay at the Frontier Rifles Mess. I had a proper bedroom with all mod cons (Indian style). There were excellent meals and some younger officers of about my own age. There was also a piano in the Mess. What seemed even more remarkable in that bare rocky region was a beautiful green English lawn, kept in perfect condition. I thought I might have a chance some day of accompanying a small expedition into the Hills. It was not to be. I had only been there a week when I had orders to return to Bengal at once, and to proceed to Chittagong, just about the furthest place in Bengal from Miranshah. However, before I left, I managed to have a sing-song, which may not have been very musical but it was certainly very lusty. And that ended my Army Career – not one that was distinguished nor one that was helpful for my duties in the ICS, but I was grateful for the experiences and the opportunity of visiting parts of India which would have remained unknown to me during my years of Service. And there I should end my account of my days in the Army, but I must add the tale of the journey from Miranshah to Calcutta (approximately 1,300 miles), which took all of five and a half days.

Day 1: Left Miranshah for Banur by road, arriving there before noon. I stayed at the Engineers' Mess. In the afternoon I met Walter Jenkins, an old friend whom I knew in Dacca. He too was to return to Civil Duty and suggested we travel together if I spent the next day in Banur, and he fixed up accommodation at the Mess where he had been staying.

Day 2: In Banur. Heard for the first time that it was public knowledge there that Sinclair had withheld report of my recurrent malaria so that he could return home. General opinion of him was as low as mine. Nonetheless, I think the fierce cold of Khajuri did finally cure me of the fever.

Day 3: Left Banur with Walter Jenkins. Was given a send-off with the knowledge that the sing-song had been enjoyed by the General. Crossed Indus in the evening and entrained for Rawalpindi.

Day 4: Arrived at Pindi too late to catch train for Calcutta, so had to spend the whole day there. Rawalpindi is a Cantonment with wide streets and neat bungalows with gardens. There was nothing to interest two travellers stranded there. To avoid complete boredom we went to the cinema in the afternoon and saw a film with Sarah Bernhardt (silent of course). The waiting room was equipped with canvas campbeds – missed trains must be a usual occurrence.

Day 5: Awoke at 5.00 for the Calcutta train, but it was several hours late. Had to change at Delhi. Baggage went in another train, but we were informed it would turn up at Moghul Serai.

Day 6: Arrived at Moghul Serai just an hour after the train we had to catch had gone. Another long wait at Moghul Serai – a very depressing Railway Settlement. Baggage had turned up. Wired friends in Calcutta with whom I was to stay – was going to arrive that day in the late afternoon or evening. Calcutta train arrived.

Day 7: Train made no effort to make up time, instead lost time all the way and, by afternoon, it was certain that it would not arrive until midnight. Wired friends to expect me next day. Reached Howrah Station at 11.30 p.m. Great Eastern Hotel full, also Grand and Spencers. Secured accommodation in the Continental in Chowringhee – very much the last resort before utter despair and sleeping on the Maidan!

Day 8: When we saw the condition of the beds, decided to leave the Continental as quickly as possible. Friends said they would return at midnight.

Next day I went to the Races. Did make some rupees, but wish I had followed my hunches. I would have laid the foundation for a future fortune!

The following day I went to a Thé Dansant at Pelitis (Firpos in those days did not have the cachet it later acquired). On the tenth day I left for Chittagong to begin work in earnest as Assistant Magistrate.

It was many moons before I had any recognition of my claim for Travelling Allowance for that long journey and it only came because, in desperation at having no reply to any of my letters, I wrote on Club notepaper from the US (United Services) Club when I was staying there for my Departmental Examination. Even after that, months were to pass before I had the money.

1920: Sub-Divisional Officer, Sirajganj

When, after retiring, they published memories of their work and life in India, Members of the Service always seemed to recall with special affection the times they spent as Sub-Divisional Officers or Magistrates. These posts offered them more opportunities of coming in closer contact with the ordinary villagers and cultivators, who constitute at least 90 per cent of the population of the country, than they ever had when they later progressed to become District Magistrates, and even Secretaries to the Government of a Province. In a Sub-Division an Officer had first hand experience in exercising the powers that had been vested in him. It is an experience that no one easily forgets.

Unfortunately I have no such rosy reminiscences of the months when I was a Sub-Divisional Officer and, for that, the Government of Bengal

Treasury Guard

was responsible. I was very pleased when in Selkenbrand Camp I received the formal notice of my posting as SDO Sirajganj because, after Narayangang, Sirajganj was the most important centre for jute in the Province, and some of the big Calcutta jute ferries would have purchasing agencies there. I would not be the sole European in the Station, and I should have a chance of having some bridge (it was the old fashioned Auction then) and some tennis. There was, I heard, a Club – a small Club perhaps, but it would be a useful meeting place after a day's work.

Before I went there, I had to spend a day or two in Calcutta getting some sticks of furniture for my bungalow, because my predecessor was not leaving anything which I could buy. I did not go to the Stores but to the shops in Row Bazaar, where everything was much cheaper and more utilitarian. They were just sticks of furniture, but they served their purpose at the time, and that was all.

When I got to Sirajganj, Roxburgh, from whom I was taking over, told me that work was heavy but not unduly so. Government had quite recently transferred one of the Deputy Magistrates, but with the promise of a replacement very soon. I was to begin my duties in my first independent charge with one Deputy short. Of the two that remained one was old and not particularly efficient, though he did his quota of case work, and the other was young and active but with little experience.

For the first week or two I was busy feeling my way, and trying to make the bungalow look habitable, which was not too easy with such furniture as I had acquired and then, instead of sending the promised replacement, Government transferred the older of the Deputies to relieve a Magistrate who had suddenly taken leave on grounds of ill health. There was again the promise of an early replacement.

So I, a complete novice, and the young Deputy with little experience, were left to cope with the work for which the Staff sanctioned by Government was the SDO and three Deputies. It was the hot weather at its most trying, and the busy season for the purchase of jute was approaching. The Government Treasury, for which I and the Deputy were responsible, was required to hold the large stocks of money which would be required by the firms for their business. There was no Bank in Sirajganj, as might have been expected. In spite of repeated reminders, no relief was sent by Government during all the time I was SDO there.

We managed to get through all the work and accumulation of arrears but, for sure, it was slog, slog, slog every day from 8.00 a.m. (when callers would begin to arrive at the bungalow) until 6.30 p.m. or 7.30 p.m. and hours later for the young Deputy. I did, however, manage to squeeze in a quick rubber or two of very poor bridge after hours. The Club, such as it was – a tin shed of two rooms, one for bridge and one for billiards – was not a stone's throw from the Courts.

One case I do remember out of the many that came before me. It was a Committal for Murder, arising out of a feud over a few acres of sandy land. I began to hear the evidence in the afternoon of a very hot summer day and, when they came to describe the injuries in pathological detail (all to be recorded in equal detail by me), I began to feel the heat. In order not to be bowled over by the heat and the murder, I called for a break, and went to the bungalow which adjoined the Offices for tea. That saved my face. When I returned I was able to cope with whatever nastiness the Court Inspector wanted to be recorded as evidence for the Prosecution; but I had already heard the most horrid bits.

It was in Sirajganj as SDO that I first began to smoke. I found cigarettes did relieve the tension that worried me when the pressure of work was heavier than usual, but I also appreciated their usefulness in my contacts with the visitors (all Bengalis) who came to see me on

The miniature line for the Canal with Donald on a trolley

90

business. If they were offered a cigarette they talked more freely, and often gave me some very helpful information. There was one problem family, Hindus of the very highest caste and the most rigid orthodoxy, who told me many things about the District and the Sub-Divisions which I was glad to hear, but only after they had a smoke. However, they never let the cigarettes touch their mouths or lips. The cigarette would be held between the third and fourth fingers, and would be brought up to the face and held near to the mouth, but so that the cigarette would not actually touch the lips. If it had, they would be defiled and have to be purified by ritual. There would be a deep intake of breath and some intake of smoke. Not very much, if any, was inhaled. After the effect of that had subsided, there would be another deep intake of breath. They must have had some satisfaction because then they would begin to talk.

In addition to what duties had to be performed in the Court and the various Offices of the Sub-Division, I was expected to spend ten days each month on tour to hear complaints, and generally get to know the common people in the villages. Needless to say, with only one deputy to help me, I could not leave headquarters as often as I should have done, and out of the tours that I did manage, two remain in my mind most vividly.

The first was to a place to the west of the Sub-Division called Taragh. It was not readily accessible in the cold weather, when such roads as there were were under water or deep in mud. However, I was told that there were police matters which should receive my attention, and so I decided that it must be visited before the full effect of the monsoons would isolate it from the remainder of the Sub-Division. Such touring as I had done in Settlement with Tom Ellis was a simple matter: one asked for some cartman to come, and come they did, and were grateful for a very small remuneration – a few annas or so.

In Sirajganj the local inhabitants would not do any work they considered beneath their dignity, and that included road maintenance and carting. The rates demanded seemed extremely high, but had to be accepted if I were to carry out my planned inspection. Bargaining over the rates occupied more time than I liked, and it was not until early afternoon that I could start. When we were what I thought would be an hour's distance from Taragh, the cartman told me that the direct road was quite impassable for carts, but that there was another way (which was much longer) by which Taragh could be reached, but not until nearly midnight. I was impatient and determined to get to that village before nightfall, so I told the cartman and servants that they could take the long road if they wanted, and I would go on alone. I had not gone far along the road when I realized that I had made a mistake. The road was muddy, and was under water in places and, when I was in sight of Taragh, it was completely submerged. There was nothing to do except go on – till the water reached my knees. I was becoming anxious when, suddenly, the sky turned black and there was such rain as I had never seen before and have never seen since. It was so heavy and so dense that I seemed to be caught in a fog. I could not see my hand if I stretched out my arm. I could only stand still and wait until the storm passed. I do not know how long it lasted but, at the time, it seemed almost interminable. When at last it ceased night had already fallen and, in such darkness, I could not press forward. I saw water snakes swimming about, and that alarmed me, though I was later told that they were harmless.

Then, at a very short distance, I noticed some huts which seemed to be rising out of the water, as they had been erected on little artificial mounds. As soon as I was near enough I shouted and, for a moment or two, there was no response. At last a man appeared at the door of the hut with a hurricane lamp, afraid at hearing such shouting during the night, though it was not very late. He was surprised to see a white stranger and asked what I wanted. I explained I was the Magistrate and wanted to go to the Police Station at Taragh and that I had been caught in the rain – and could he help me. That he was most willing to do. He told me to wait while he fetched his boat. It was little bigger than a 'dugout' and, to my mind, quite as unsteady. He held the boat while I settled myself gingerly into a sitting position at the end of the boat. I tried, as far as possible, to remain absolutely still. While he paddled along he recounted his surprise at hearing the sound of a voice calling for assistance out of the darkness. As we approached another hut, it was his turn to shout, but the answering call did not come as soon as he wanted, so he shouted again and, when the occupant of the hut appeared, he explained that he was taking the Magistrate to the Police Station. He had heard my voice and came to see what he should do. It was a brief, accurate and factual narrative, and I could be seen as corroboration of what he had been saying. The two of them had a short conversation which I could not follow before we set off again.

He had to stop and hail the occupants of the next huts which we came to but, by this time, his imagination had been roused. Facts were not sufficient for his tale. He dramatized his doubts and fears when he heard a voice in the darkness, and he made a very impressive story of it – and here he was taking the Magistrate to the Police Station. There was another hut just a short way off, and again there was a stop, and the occupant was called to witness the Magistrate being taken to the Police Station. His tale had to be repeated with even more dramatization of how he had felt and what I was supposed to have said. I began to wonder if I had actually said what he put into my mouth.

There was one other hut to be passed before we actually arrived at the centre of Taragh and the Police Station. This was his last opportunity to tell of my rescue and he excelled himself. His description of his doubts and fears and his surprise became more vivid and more dramatic, but more unreal. It was not a shout that he had heard but a pitiful cry for help from a person in great distress. He could tell a most convincing story, though most of it was fiction. I don't think he appreciated that most of what he said was not the truth but what he had imagined. Yet there was truth at the heart of his story. I was grateful to the man for his willing and ready assistance, and for the enlightenment I gained of how the mind of the illiterate Bengali works, and the difficulty in separating the truth from the maze of imagined additions grafted on it in any verbal account. As Taragh was in a very isolated locality and therefore infrequently subject to official inspection, the Sub-Inspector of Police in charge of the Station had a power amongst his people not held by Sub-Inspectors in other areas so I think my saviour was pleased to be brought to his notice for the assistance given to me.

I had not been expected, but the Inspection Room was soon made ready and, as everything I was wearing was soaking, I was glad to take the offer of a dhoti while my togs were being dried. I did not attempt to wear the dhoti Bengali fashion, draped round my legs. I treated it more as a Roman toga, and in this style it was very comfortable. I was given some Bengali food, which I was only too glad to accept, and was soon asleep without waiting for the arrival of the servants with the cart and my bedding roll. Next morning I was told that they had arrived at 2.00 a.m. I can't remember anything about the Inspection that I undertook in Taragh, how long I stayed there (I only intended to remain for two nights at most) or about the return journey. It must have been uneventful.

The other memory of my touring is of an entirely different character. I was to spend about four days in the North of the Sub-Division, some fifteen or twenty miles from headquarters and, as the road was good, not likely to be muddy or submerged, I rode there. Some eight to ten miles along the road I passed a horse which had fallen and could not rise. Its hind legs had given way, but its forelegs were braced as if in an attempt to rise. Probably it had cumray, a disease which was common in the area, and for which there was no cure. One of the gate-men had lost two horses that season: they had to be shot. This animal had been left to die by the roadside. It had given up trying to rise; its great eyes seemed fixed on nothingness – but it was still alive. When I returned four days later where the horse had been, there was its skeleton with the bones of the front legs braced to rise and the bones of the hind legs bent on the ground. It was the skeleton of the animal just as I had seen it in life – nothing had moved. There was not a strip of flesh left: and as there had been some rain, the bones had been washed to whiteness.

I covered my eyes and hurried on, and tried not to think of the heartlessness of the people of this country, where death is so common. But I can still see that horse by the roadside, and the skeleton.

I had been some four months in Sirajganj when I received a letter asking if I would be willing to go as Assistant Settlement Officer in the Settlement Operations, which were due to start in the Districts of Patna and Bogra after the Pujahs. In those days it was considered something of an honour to be selected for Settlement work and, as I had enjoyed the four months I had spent in Bankina at the Settlement Group working with several other ICS people of the same seniority as me, I wrote accepting. I knew there would be little social life in either district, but that lack would be compensated for by the freedom I would have in the work. I have never regretted my choice. I gained a greater facility in speaking the Bengali of the peasants, and a greater understanding of their ways and problems. In their disputes over land or anything else, hearing them say their say without the intervention of lawyers, I could discover more quickly and I believe with more reliability, who was lying and what was true.

But what I am certain did me more good was that I had to spend some twenty days in the month riding across fields to inspect the accuracy of field plans which were being plotted for the Food Settlement Maps. Later in the season I also had to ascertain that the names of everyone who had an interest in the land and the amount of rent or remuneration they were under obligation to pay, were correctly recorded. Galloping across the open fields in the cold weather of Bengal was exhilarating. The days were not too hot, and the weather was dry and sunny, and to spend most of the day in the open for my work was a joy. I gathered strength from the experience.

There were still a few weeks, however, before I could make over charge to my successor as SDO. They did not slip pleasurably by. I had gone to see Kelly, the Missionary for the Australian Baptists, when he asked me to have a meal with him on Saturday evening and remain with him until after dinner on Sunday. He said it would be good for me to get away from the bungalow even for one night. The bungalow was next door to the Courts and Offices, and he thought living so close to my work was getting me down. At any rate I would be relieved of the Sunday callers if I accepted, which I gladly did. I had not thought I was looking care-worn or harassed by my work, but there must have been symptoms.

It was a very super meal that was served – and much superior to what my cook provided. I had been afraid that, as I would be staying over Sunday, there might be more religion that I was accustomed to. But apart from Grace before meals – and one prayer – there was no religious talk, and I enjoyed my weekend away from home very much. It was a very kindly invitation, and only the first of many occasions when I had to be grateful to the Kellys and the other Australian Baptist Missionaries with whom I came into contact, for their understanding, advice and help.

On the Monday back in Court I felt fresher, but on Thursday there was a little red spot on my forehead. On Friday it began to swell, and by Saturday I could hardly see out of my eyes. On the Sunday the

Donald on horseback

95

Bengali Assistant Surgeon said there could be no more delay. He came to the bungalow, my bed was brought on to the verandah, the servants got ready boiling water for sterilization, and the Assistant Surgeon lanced the carbuncle. He made a thoroughly good job of it, but I had no anaesthetics, and the orderlies said my shouts could be heard as far as 'Karta Khal', a canal which had been dug. That, I believe, is an exaggeration, but I did scream. Vestiges of the cut can be seen on my forehead to this day.

I spent the next three days in Purdah, then took Court for the remainder of the week, but only doing light duties. As I had heard nothing from my successor, I went to Darjeeling for ten days' casual leave, to which I was entitled. With a deep bandage round my head I looked a fit case for hospitalization. However, that was not necessary, and I went back to Sirajganj feeling refreshed, only to find a letter from Davis who was to take over, grumbling at not knowing when he could come. I was annoyed because, if he had written to me when he heard of his posting, I would have received the letter before I set off for Darjeeling – and I should have stayed for a few days longer and enjoyed a good three weeks in the cool air of the hills, as well as saving the second rail fare to Darjeeling, a not inconsiderable sum.

He was one of those people who have very liberal views, but was much less tolerant of the Bengalis than I ever was. He had come to Dacca the year I did, caught dysentery and had been in England for more than two years on leave. He did not stay in Sirajganj very long before returning to England, where he became a cleric – a more suitable vocation for him. He certainly proved a very bad bargain for the Secretary of State. He was very awkward to deal with regarding the handing over of charge and buying such furniture as I did not want, for he had none of his own, and there was none to be had in Sirajganj. Being SDO no longer and with no place in the town where I could stay, I returned to Darjeeling for the Pujahs and complete recovery before joining the Settlement Operations which were about to start in Patna.

1921: Bogra (Settlement)

There is an airfield now in Bogra, if not an airport, but in the twenties Bogra was a small station for Christians who had fallen from Grace, where they would have time to meditate on the advantages and merits of conformity. The town was uninteresting and depressing: there were no suitable houses, the streets were narrow, and shops where one could get anything except rice and dahl were just non-existent. There were the American Missionaries (husband and wife) who tried to be friendly, but were so fundamentalist in their beliefs that the Magistrate, a promoted Deputy, asked me if I really could believe the earth was made in seven days, as they apparently did.

The surroundings of the town were equally depressing, because the fields with the raised earth for the castor oil plant, on the leaves of which the silkworms fed, had been neglected since the collapse of the industry in the middle of the last century.

But at one time, certainly over a thousand years ago, it had been a prosperous place, and the Capital of Bengal, though there were no traces of houses, only a great embankment, which popularly was said to have been built by a legendary giant. And there were stories of a Merchant Prince, whose name is for evermore recalled in folklore. The only relics of these times were the broken statues of the Gods of a very extensive Pantheon, which was to be found outside the village. The reception given to the Settlement Operations was such that no one of the officials had time for anything except getting the work started, and the armies given some security.

There was always great apparent confusion at the start of the first season's work in any area. There never was any timetable for the allocation of duties. The amins knew when the field work was due to

Surveying

97

start, and made their own arrangements for coming. Usually they all came on the same day to get their orders and collect the planning tables, the measuring posts, and the 22 yd. chain and other implements. Then they left with their assistants (usually a young relation) before aiming for the villages where they would have to find accommodation while they plotted the boundaries of the fields on the maps they were preparing. But in October 1921 they found problems in the villages, and some who had gone ahead of the others returned to tell of the opposition they had encountered. No shelter could be found, every door was closed to them, and they were debarred from buying any food in the markets or the village shops. Few of them had cash to tide them over more than the first day or two, and they soon ran out of money to pay the extortionate prices asked for something to eat. They were very poorly paid at the best of times. I often wondered why they came back year after year to doss down in uncomfortable huts, after dragging a chain across fields in the heat of the day. This year they did endure hardship. After most of them had at last departed, Philpot (he was Settlement Officer) and I had to go out ourselves to see the conditions in the villages, and we had to take with us supplies of money to help those amins who had spent everything they had brought with them.

Our first stop was at a place called Mokumtola, where there was a Dak Bungalow, a dispensary and nothing else – not even a shop or a Police Outpost. However, it was at a crossroads and Philpot went to

Crossing the river

the West and I went to the East. It was tiring going along those narrow village paths on a cycle, and a thankless task meeting several of the amins who, unable to begin work, were dossing down in great discomfort and in need of money, which I was able to give them. However, they were prepared to stay on in the hope that times would improve when the villagers came to know them better. Towards the end of the afternoon I heard of a large market that was meeting on the day that I was doing this round. I decided to go there myself. It was farther than I had been led to believe, and darkness was beginning to close in when I reached it. Flares were already being lit. I parked my cycle by a tree, and went forward. I had not reached the nearest stall when a crowd rushed at me shouting. I could not hear what they were saying, but they came waving lathis and one, who was stronger than the others, hit me twice with a heavy oar. My topee was knocked off at the first blow, but the second caught me on the back of the head and I turned to run, blood streaming from the cut. I managed to find shelter in a hut. After I had been hit, the crowd's anger seemed to abate. I waited in this hut, however, until it was quite dark before leaving as quickly as I could and, collecting my cycle, found my way to the main road. It was a main road for Bogra but, after the rains, it was little better than a wide deeply rutted cart-track, and Mokumtola and the Dak Bungalow were, as I learned later, only four miles distant. As I trudged along with the cycle, I feared I would never reach them. The night was pitch black and I could not see where the road began and the verges (such as they were) ended. I often stumbled into a deep rut, having missed the well-trodden centre of the road at a particularly dark spot. My head throbbed with the blow I had had, and my whole body ached.

I have no idea how long I took to do those four miles, and Philpot was relieved to see me arrive – whole. He gave me a very stiff whisky (I could have done with one even stiffer), got me to bed and called the Sub-Assistant Surgeon from the dispensary nearby. He was most efficient and tidied up my head with a very wide bandage. I got to bed again but, after an hour or more, was wakened to give my statement to the local Sub-Inspector of Police, who had been called from the Thana (Police Station), at Siliguri, a mile and a half away. I think it was sufficiently detailed but, to his disappointment, I had to admit that owing to the darkness, the crowd and the speed with which everything happened, I could not recognise any of my assailants.

After that I had a quiet sleep for the remainder of the night and, in the morning, felt fit enough to agree to accompany Philpot and the young Deputy Magistrate when they went out to take stock of the situation – not on cycles, nor on foot but on horseback. Most unusually there was nobody about on the roads. When we reached a wide expanse of fields – more than two miles wide, I should say –from which the crops had been harvested, there was nobody to be seen working, digging the soil or gleaning some fallen grains of paddy. We had come to assess the mood of the people, and so headed towards the only place where there was existence of habitation. It turned out to be a great barn and, when we neared it, we could see through the wide open door a huddle of stalwart villagers, most of them very stalwart, deep in conversation and very excited. Much more ominous, however, was a large stack of thick and stout long lathis each sharpened to a spear-like point. They looked very dangerous and quite lethal. We could not risk an encounter – one glance was sufficient – so we turned the horses to leave as quietly as possible. But there must have been some noise, or there may have been one of the band on the lookout, because they soon began to come out of the barn, each armed with one of the stakes, and moved very fast in our direction. However, their speed was rather limited by the fact that they had to keep to the narrow field boundary, which was raised just a few inches above the earth. That was the only path they could take. We prodded the horses to make them move faster, without urging them to a run, because we were most anxious that we did not appear to have been put to flight. When we had reached a road and

Donald's horse in the boat and his chaprassi *waiting to get on with his bicycle*

out-distanced our pursuers, then and then only did we let the horses trot and make for Mokumtola.

There had been no incident, but the hostility and danger were apparent. Somehow one could cope with these during the hours of daylight, but the nights were much more ominous. The air was filled with the throbbing of drums, from which there was no relief. In the darkness one could see the villages ablaze with light when, ordinarily, a dim hurricane lamp might be the only perceptible illumination. Flares were moving about while the drums throbbed incessantly. One village would call to another by drums, and the other would answer back. The drums conveyed a message; what it was we could not understand, except that it was not friendly to us. At times the drumbeat was used to rouse the blood and excite the spirit of violence.

Night after night there was no respite from the drums and then, suddenly, they ceased, clearly on instructions from outside the district because such objections as the villagers might have had at the onset of Settlement remained unchanged. I found out one day when I had to cycle in from Mokumtola to Bogra eight miles away that there was some method of sending messages from village to village over the air. A few young agitators saw me depart, and I was met at Bogra by some young men who had been alerted to my coming. There was of course no telephone, and the drums had been silent.

There were two other occasions on which I was assaulted. Of the first I remember little except that my assailant was known and brought to trial. On the second I was attacked by clods of earth thrown at me. Those I managed to avoid by adroit change of the horse's direction. My recollection of the trial in the other case is of being asked by the lawyer for the accused if I had used some vituperation and disgraceful names to the accused. When I denied this allegation, a certified copy of my statement to the police was produced, and I realised what I had actually said. The copyist had misread my handwriting. My remarks had been quite unexceptional.

After about a fortnight the agitation began to die down, and the amins became able to begin work in earnest. The people were a trifle restless and the amins had to be given financial support, sometimes from my own pocket, to keep them from leaving. However, in spite of all the trouble that they had given, I found the people of Bogra more friendly than those of Patna. Before peace was finally in order, there was one occasion when I was returning to my headquarters in the early afternoon, when I heard a shout. 'Where do you think you are going?

101

Is it to the *bil*?' (a watery marsh). Of course it was not. I wanted the Dak Bungalow. In Patna I would have been allowed to reach the marsh, which would have proved very difficult for the horse to negotiate. In Patna, if I asked a direction the answer was always, 'I don't know.' I was never sure whether this ignorance was due to lack of knowledge, lack of interest or a sheer desire to be obstructive.

Naturally enough, I searched the columns of the *Statesman* and the *Englishman* for any reference to the attack upon myself, but there was none. However, my father noticed a short paragraph in the *Scotsman* that a Donald MacPherson of the ICS had been attacked during Settlement Week. He wired the India Office, and received a reassuring telegram. I am unsure whether there was any notice in the Indian papers, such as the *Amrita Bazaar Patrika*. Manipulation of the Press? The old missionary lady I had met in the depths of a jungly village in Patna was told I had been assaulted and killed, and I believe similar exaggerations were current in many parts of the two districts.

The name of the market where I was attacked was Dakumara – Defeat of the Dacoits – and was so called to commemorate a victory over the Dacoits by a contingent of the Forces of the East India Company under the command of Major Rennell, who was wounded in the fight. The Dacoits, or Sanyassis, came down from the foothills of the Himalayas in very cold weather. They assembled at a notable outpost in Bogra and roamed the countryside of North Bengal extorting money from the villages and, at times, being bought off with huge sums of money by the Collectors of the Districts under the East Indian Company. This victory seems to have been decisive in breaking the powers of the Dacoits. Major Rennell was the great cartographer of Eastern India.

I find I have forgotten to mention one memorable occasion. The hostility was beginning to die down, but there was still restiveness in some of the Eastern villages, and a small body of armed police was dispatched to the area to allay the tension. It was felt that their presence would have a pacifying effect, as they would stay in the villages and make friends with the people. At the slightest hint of trouble reinforcements would be sent out under the command of an officer, who could shoulder responsibility for punitive action. On the day they were to leave I went out to one of the largest of the villages, hoping they would be there before I arrived. They had been delayed, so I was met by a band of the villagers. They had probably heard that the armed police were on the way, because information of that sort would be passed on the village wireless messages. They were not obstructive. However, they were not friendly, though they were prepared to speak. I could listen, but I could also speak, and speak I did for one whole hour until I could see the police approaching. Never have I spoken such fluent Bengali as I did that day. I was reaching the end of anything to say, and was becoming rather desperate and hoarse, when the relief arrived. But I had accomplished what I wanted. I held their attention, and did not touch on the political situation. I spoke chiefly, I think, on crops and the diseases from which most of them suffered. At any rate, when I left, they were good enough to give me quite a friendly send-off.

A month or so after peace had been restored, I happened to stand under a big tree for shade and saw, lying among the roots, a large statue. The head and most of the body were in perfect condition, but the legs were not to be found. It was one of the loveliest sculptures I had seen in India. Its face had the serenity of those Renaissance Madonnas – so very unusual among the Indian deities. There must have been an important building at or near this place, but all trace of it had vanished. The solitary tree stood in open fields stretching for two or three miles. The nearest habitation was a good three quarters of a mile away, and there was no road nearby. I wish now that I had thought to have it moved to some place of safety, but it would have been a problem trying to arrange transport.

A year later I enquired about the feasibility of getting cartage for it, but was told that some zealot had smashed it to smithereens. After seeing that statue I began to look more carefully at the broken black stone images to be found in the outskirts of many of the villages. Most had been damaged to such an extent that their preservation was not worth while, but there were a few I thought ought to be in museums, and I arranged for them to be sent off. Two of the larger statues were to go to the Indian Museum in Calcutta, which had the most comprehensive collection of these sculptures, and two smaller statues to the Barind Research Society's Museum in Rajshali, which specialized in statues from North Bengal. In none of them that I sent had the figure of the God been mutilated. I thought this should be the chief criterion for selecting statues for display in a museum. A gallery of these black stone figures can be depressing, if the images are not in good condition, and the deity so defaced as not to be readily recognisable. I think I made a good choice, because Dr Bhattachaufa from Rajshali, and now Curator of the Indian Antiquities Section of the Museum in Berlin, recognised one of the statues that I had sent to the Research Society. He had seen it as a student in Rajshali.

There was some bother over one of the statues because, as soon as I began to notice it, some villagers laid claim to it, as their family god. The headdress and the necklace were brightened with gold paint, and the eyelids of the eyes were emphasised with white paint. In doing this they made this quite lovely figure very tawdry. The Karingo, however, carried out my instruction, and had the figure sent away to Rajshali. For this action these people approached the District Magistrate accusing the Karingo of theft of the god. The Magistrate, who was a Bengali, a promoted Deputy, showed them no sympathy. The Deity was Brahma, who had ceased many years ago to attract the devotion and prayers of the people. He had been left lying in the open, subject to all the elements, neglected and uncared for until I had him moved to a safer place.

I visited Bogra in 1924 and Rajshali in 1925, when I went to the Barind Society's Museum, but was never told of the discovery of a gold covered statue in what had been the capital town one thousand years ago. After the interest that I had shown, I think I should have been told of it then. I saw the statue only when I was inspecting as Excise Commissioner and was struck by its beauty. The Research Society had been most secretive and possessive about the statue. I cannot understand the reason, because it is probably the first thing of its kind in Bengal. Rajshali is now in Bangla Desh. The existence of this statue is known only to a few scholars. Even the India Office Library Records were in ignorance of it, and were refused a photograph of it when they did request one.

1928: Disaster at New Birbhum Coal Company

In 1988 I had an unexpected reminder of Asansol and coal mines when my wife and I went to see lawyers after her great-aunt's death, and he read out the list of Companies in India in which she had held shares. Amongst them there was the New Birbhum Coal Company, which had been the cause of a serious disaster in its neighbouring mine, belonging to another Coal Company. The circumstances were exceptional and, because the Chief Inspector of Mines (the Office who ordinarily deals with the conduct of these Official Enquiries) had himself been to the mines the previous day and I would therefore be an important witness I, as District Magistrate of Burdwan, was saddled with the responsibility. I was most surprised when I was informed of the task because, as District Magistrate, I thought I should have been informed of the disaster which had occurred a few months previously. The loss of life had been heavy and I was even more surprised that I had seen no reference to it in the *Statesman* nor in the *Amrita Bazaar Patrika*, which was not well-disposed to European internal management. One hundred and thirty three people were drowned in a rush of water, from which they had no chance of escape. Nowadays, even in *The Times*, I see reports from faraway countries of accidental disasters of two or three in some factory or river. A disaster of over a hundred would be given at least some special prominence, if only for a day.

I did not make any comment when I heard what the lawyer had read out. His brother had been in coal in India. Under Balmer Lawries he might have been the Manager of the New Birbhum Colliery at the time, and perhaps a reference to the enquiry might not have been appreciated. All mining interests had been nationalized, so the connection had been broken.

Taking evidence can be boring at the best of times, but technical evidence lacks the human interest, and can be deadly dull. Besides my colleagues on the enquiry, being engineers, would pursue irrelevancies. Five days of this, at the expense of my normal duties, was annoying. Representatives of the Managing Agents in Calcutta also attended to safeguard their interests.

The facts which were established were so unusual that I have remembered them very clearly after sixty years, though some small details may be wrong. The country around Asansol is quite undulating and, in consequence, the New Birbhum coal mine was a little higher than that of the other company. The seams were also very slightly tilted. They were not narrow like many of the seams in the country when the miners had to hack out the coal, some from a recumbent position. When I was taken down one of the mines so that I could more readily appreciate what had happened, I was surprised at the spaciousness of the workings.

There were two seams in the New Birbhum Mine and, after a fire in the lower seam, it had been closed and blocked off. Fire, however, had started in the upper seam and, in an attempt to extinguish it, a continuous stream of water was being pushed down. The Chief Inspector of Mines came and inspected the work and was apparently satisfied; he did not anticipate any danger to the other mine, nor did he consider the amount of water used to flood the seam unusual. However, much of the water had not gone to the seam where the fire was, but had poured down the main shaft.

As I mentioned, the other mine was at a slightly lower level and, like the New Birbhum Mine, was very close to the border between the two villages. At the lower levels the workings of the two mines had become dangerously near to each other. Instead of a wall of coal not less than thirty feet thick separating the two workings, the partition was only a few feet thick and not strong enough to withstand the pressure of the water that had been building up in the New Birbhum Mine. When, years ago, the lower seam had been blocked off, the lower seam in the other mine had been abandoned, but there had been a stopper in the shaft. When the water from the New Birbhum Mine burst through the partition and into the other mine, it was forced up the shaft in the other mine. When it reached the upper seam, on account of the tilt, it poured into the seam where men were working. It was like a wall of water; the men were taken unawares and had no chance to resist its force and escape.

The danger of serious accidents when two contiguous mines were working on the same seam had been recognised by the Mines Department under the Government of India. They had ruled that there should be no working to within fifteen feet of the village border. If both companies complied with this ruling, it would amount to a substantial barrier of about thirty feet of coal. To ensure observance, there had been a further instruction that the fifteen feet be indicated on the plans of the mine. Both Mine Managers had faithfully carried out the necessary protection measures as they saw it. Unfortunately, when the mining leases were negotiated from the landlords, what was known as the 'Thak' maps were used. These were preliminary plans for the preparation of the Definitive Maps of the villages, under Ordnance Survey. In some districts the 'Thak' maps had fairly accurate representations of the village boundaries and could reasonably have been used in the granting of any privilege. In the Asansol area the 'Thak' maps were merely rough sketches of the lie of the land, often wildly inaccurate, and with little relevance to conditions above ground.

Inevitably, if the 'Thak' maps of two contiguous villages were compared, it would be seen that there were overlaps of quite considerable areas. But, whether for greed or from ignorance it was these inaccurate and misleading maps which were used as the basis of these two mines. The 'Thak' map of each mine covered a large stretch of land of the other, and the fifteen feet line on each was actually within the boundary of the other.

In his Settlement Report of the Asansol Area, taken in conjunction with the Bankura District, the risk of a disaster from this abuse of the 'Thak' maps was clearly set out by F.W. Robertson, who was very critical of both the landlords and the Mine Companies – and that was ten years previously. No notice had been taken of his advice, and the Mines Department had certainly not bothered about them.

In writing the Report I had the assistance of the Chief Inspector of Mines on the technical issues but, on the 'rights' of the Companies, I could only advise that the Official Settlement Maps of the various villages be shown on the Mining Plans – their working Plans. If this were done, the Inspector of Mines could readily determine where danger lay and take some action. I had to finish the Report after I left Burdwan, and have no knowledge of whether my recommendations were acted upon or not. From the circumstances of this disaster, I believe there is a chance that the Government of India heeded them.

1928: Dr Tomb

Throughout the year I was at Burdwan one case, above all others, gave me persistent worry. Yet I might have saved myself these months of anxiety had I not acted against my better judgement and gone out of my way to help (so I thought) a man who came to me for assistance.

Burdwan sports, Donald on right, wearing shorts

He was at his wit's end to know what to do as he had discovered that he had been cheated. He could not estimate the extent of his loss as he was about to go on home leave and all the arrangements had been made and could not be altered so near to his date of departure.

The Asansol Mine's Board of Health was frequently in the news, and always with the most favourable notice of the work of its Medical Officer, who ensured that it received the widest publicity. I was aware that the Chief Medical Officer in the Bengal Health Department, Dr Bentley, did not share the general opinion of Dr Tomb's achievements, but I attributed that to the professional jealousy which so often afflicts experts of profound but differing ideas on the same subject. When he heard that I was to go to Burdwan, my first Collector, who had also been in Burdwan, wrote that I must make a friend of Dr Tomb, a man of integrity, who had developed the Mine's Board of Health from practically nothing, and had wiped out the scourge of malaria from the minefield. And Donovan, who had done a stint at the Department of Health in Delhi, said one of those Roving Commissioners from the League of Nations had visited the Mine's Board of Health during a Tour of India, and was enthusiastic about all that had been seen. Naturally, I looked forward to making Dr Tomb's acquaintance.

I did not visit Asansol for the Monthly Meeting of the Mine's Board of Health (as District Magistrate I was Chairman) till I had been in the District for some weeks and, by that time, the hot weather had begun in earnest. Asansol lies at the fringe of the Central India Plain or Plateau, when in the summer the temperature rises to over 100 degrees for weeks at a stretch and often touches 110 or 115 degrees. Consequently, office hours were from 6.30 or thereabouts until 11.00 or 12 noon.

The Mine's Board Meeting was at 8.00 a.m., and all the members except for me and Dr Tomb were Mine Managers. There were about eight, I think. Dr Tomb was going on leave the next day. The Meeting was brief, ending, naturally enough, with good wishes for the voyage etc. After the Meeting I felt I was getting a touch of the sun and was preparing to return home as soon as I could, and was surprised to see Dr Tomb coming to the Dak Bungalow where I was staying. He had a long story. He had allowed his clerk to keep his personal accounts and, when he was adding them up, he found the clerk had cheated him of about Rs.120. At least that is what he thought was the amount, but could not confirm it as he could not have any verification from Calcutta before he left. He sought my assistance. I did think it strange that he had allowed a clerk, even his confidential clerk, to keep his personal accounts, but accepted his word for it, as I accepted his statement that he could not verify the balance from Calcutta in time. I had been told he was a man of sterling worth, who could be relied on, and my acceptance was understandable.

However, I said I could do nothing to help him on the basis of a conversation. I needed to have some definite statement in writing before I could consider any action at all. He was most urgent that something be done, as he could not leave with his money at the mercy of the clerk. At last I agreed that, if he prepared a statement, and swore to the truth of it by affidavit, I would suspend his clerk, provided that Dr Tomb promised to send the necessary documentary corroborative evidence as soon as he reached England. He hesitated but eventually accepted these terms. I had to wait for some time for the sworn statement and, when I read it, I was disappointed to find that it was not as definite as I had expected from what he had told me in conversation. It did, however, accuse the clerk and, after some thought and renewed assurance that the documents and accounts would be sent, I suspended the clerk and returned to Burdwan before the mid-day sun.

I did not go to Asansol for another month, and then it was for the Mine's Board Meeting. I had heard nothing from Dr Tomb, but put that down to the holiday feeling. On my arrival the SDO told me that the Clerk was blaming Dr Tomb for the financial loss that had been alleged, because he had fudged the accounts. The money had not been Dr Tomb's personal cash, but money put at his disposal by the Department of Health of the Government of India for his travelling expenses in connection with some work he had been asked to undertake. I never knew what that work was, and never asked the Government of India. I was shown the accounts, however. At first, an advance of Rs.150 had been placed at his disposal, to be renewed on the supply of evidence of travelling expenditure. Money was drawn from this advance and, before the end of a month, a statement of the journeys taken – chiefly rail fares – was sent to Delhi, and a further Rs.150 was made available. None of these journeys had been undertaken; he had never left Asansol. Similarly, for the next several months there were false statements of travelling, when Dr Tomb had remained at home in Asansol, and further allotments of Rs.150 made. He was allowed to draw from these funds as required, provided that he supplied regular reports of his journeys.

Naturally I asked Dr Tomb to send me the papers he had promised from England, and let him understand that I had access to his travelling claims. I think I was polite enough, though I was beginning to lose patience. He did send me the bank account after he had been given the right to draw money direct, and not against any advance. When the bank account was checked against his travelling claim statements, the divergences were extreme. According to the claims he had gone to Dacca, while he had remained in Asansol.

When I realised what Tomb had done over these accounts, I had a look at the Asansol Diaries and became convinced that much of the work for the Mine's Board was mere eyewash. Perhaps, as a layman, it was not for me to judge – but so very little seemed to have been done.

At last Tomb decided to shorten his leave and settle accounts with me – for his letters showed that he had become hostile. He arrived just in time for the Mine's Board Meeting. I had hoped to attend, but found myself that day in the Presidency General Hospital in Calcutta. The Civil Surgeon in Burdwan had brought me in and, on my arrival, everything was in readiness to give me a saline injection and a stiff dose of quinine intravenously. The germ had left me, but I was so weak I could not stand. Round one to Tomb, who would have had the ear of the members. The Civil Surgeon was only acting under Government orders. Because of the death of the Judge from Burdwan fever a year or two previously, any official who caught this germ had to be sent at once to Calcutta, and I had caught a very dangerous attack of this potentially fatal type of malaria.

I did attend the next Meeting of the Board, and sensed that Tomb had used his opportunity to prejudice the members against me and, as I was not fully recovered, I did not attempt a confrontation. But I was worried. The Sub-Divisional Officer let me know that the Manager of the Imperial Bank in Asansol had asked him to pass on to me a warning that Tomb was gunning for me. It was all so unpleasant. Perhaps I did treat the affair too personally, because I felt that he had let me down and, by a sworn statement, had induced me to do something I should not otherwise have done. However, I could not help being anxious as I had found Tomb to be unreliable and unscrupulous.

The Meetings of the Board became tense and protracted. I asked questions and Tomb was barely polite in his replies but it was one of these, hastily given, that alerted the members to the reality behind the sham they had believed in. When he read out part of the monthly report I asked what certain figures stood for, and he quickly replied, 'They are Babu's figures.' There was a pause. I said, 'Oh!' and passed on to the next item, but he realized that he had made a mistake and was cautious.

Shortly after this I was posted to Calcutta, and I felt most strongly that I had to have this affair settled before I left. His affidavit sworn statement to me was perjury in intent if not in the most literal interpretation of what he had said, and all the subordinate staff must have been aware of the fiddle in the Government Accounts. Nor had the clerk been silent on the subject in his talks with other members of the staff!

I never asked the clerk for an explanation, but was sure that whatever he said would incriminate Tomb more surely than the records did. In such circumstances Tomb could not exercise any control of his staff. I then decided to put all the papers to the most senior member of the Board, the Superintendent of the Andrew Yates Mines. He was perturbed at what he saw. He had never had any reason to suspect Tomb's integrity, and he considered the sworn statement to be damaging in the extreme, especially as he had availed himself of the services of the clerk for his fiddle and then claimed that the clerk was responsible for the alleged failure of the accounts to balance. When I told him that Tomb said that he could not mention the exact amount of the loss because he could not have the information that he wanted from Calcutta, he just said, 'What nonsense!' Tomb had only to lift the receiver and he would have been in touch with the Calcutta Bank. Until then I had been in districts of East Bengal – east that is of the Ganges – and there had been no direct telephone contact with Calcutta. In my youthful ignorance I had believed him.

After a most protracted session this old member told me to leave the matter to him and next morning at the Meeting of the Board I heard what had happened. When I left the previous evening he had called all the other members of the Board to a special meeting in the early morning, and they had decided that Tomb could not remain and would be asked to resign. He was to be given an amount equal to what he would have paid as his contribution to a Provident Fund. Tomb had been summoned and found that all the members who, until then, had been his friends were now hostile. So he decided to accept their terms. After that the official meeting was rather an anti-climax. I was pleased at this most satisfactory result. There would be no publicity and no scandal. However when my successor, Douglas, arrived to take over charge, he shattered my equanimity by the news that Government would never sanction this arrangement. He had been Under Secretary to the

Finance Department and, therefore, spoke with authority and certainty. He was a strange person. I had known him in Edinburgh, where he read history a year or two in advance of me, but he was always impersonal. He never seemed to mix in with the others, and that characteristic he brought to Bengal. The Finance Department seemed just suited to his temperament but, seemingly, he had not fitted in. Four years later he was one of the three District Magistrates shot in Midnapur.

Wedding day

I had not been a week in Calcutta when Dr Bentley, the Director of Health, came to ask me if it was true that Tomb was leaving the Mine's Board of Health. He had not been aware of any enquiry and, though I could not definitely confirm that Tomb's resignation and the terms agreed on would be approved by the Government of Bengal, he was obviously well pleased. Contrary to what Douglas had said, the Government did approve.

A year or two later I heard that Tomb had gone to the European Association in Calcutta which had been formed, amongst other reasons, to give protection and assistance (not financial) to Europeans who had come to India under contracts of employment and felt they had suffered injustice. Apparently this Association turned down his complaint and, I believe, thought that he had been very generously treated. Still later he made a representation to the Secretary of State for India who, I think, had known of Tomb's work in Asansol, but again he had no success.

I have often wondered why, for such a small sum – about £9-£10 – and in full knowledge of his accounting irregularities, Tomb made complaint to me and asked for some action. Most men in these circumstances would have met the loss from their own pockets, and hoped that no one would suspect them of tampering with the accounts. I sometimes wonder if nothing had been said about his financial irregularities whether I should have come to distrust the value of his work and the amount of time he gave to that work. One result of this experience has been that I distrust most Health Statistics, especially those relating to preventative medicine and charitable associations.

1935: Tube Wells for Jubilee Year
Mr. John Anderson, as Governor, had let it be known through the Press that it would be fitting to honour the 25th Anniversary of King George VI's reign with some memorial. His message was in general terms, and was not followed by any concrete suggestions. I, as well as a good many other District Officers, thought of ideas that might prove popular. The provision of good drinking water seemed one that would meet with a ready response, especially as there would be a new well in each Union – rather like a parish, without the church of course. No sooner had I mentioned it than it was taken up enthusiastically by the Chairman of the District Board, and money began to come in. In fact, the collections were very good because the improvement of the Water Supply was being made into a Special Appeal associated with the

Jubilee. It would be a celebration of benefit to every part of the District. One enthusiast proposed small covered toilets to commemorate each Jubilee well!

At length Sir John Anderson let it be known that he had wanted a good new hospital for Calcutta but, by this time, in other districts besides Hooghly, the collections that had been made for local commemoratives could not be diverted to any Calcutta project, and the Calcutta scheme had to be abandoned.

So Hooghly had its tube wells, each with its cement plaque, before the Jubilee. There were no ceremonies. There were no press reports. There was, of course, no television. In the course of touring I did visit several villages where I saw the tube wells in operation. In fact they were never at rest, as long as there was light, and there was a danger that they might be worn out long before their normal life expectancy. I did drink the water without risk. What I believe was most appreciated, apart from its purity, was the feeling of coolness – it was so welcome in the heat of May.

Tube wells had been on the market for at least a decade so, in 1935, tube wells were not news, as they seemed to be in 1988 when I made a point of watching a film on TV which, from the resumé in the press, seemed to deal with measures to tackle the problems created by these disastrous floods. I did not anticipate that it would be a repeat of a general nature not dealing with the flood at all, because the showing of a controversial film had had to be postponed at the last minute.

The subject was the provision of good drinking water in the areas nearest the Bay of Bengal, and quite a drama was made of the occasion. There was a preliminary explanation stressing the value to the health of the village in this area, where much of the water was brackish, and the site seemed to have been selected more for its picturesque possibilities than for its suitability to meet the people's needs.

The boring of the well was shown, and then two or three women from some adjacent homesteads (which were not visible) were brought along. They were obviously dressed for the occasion, and had saris which must have been supplied by the TV people, because they were of a colour and standard that could never have been bought in any village shop or market. They were given to understand what the benefits of the well would be, and then an English lady came along from the right. The villagers came on from the left. The English lady was obviously devoted to welfare and must have been near at hand to appear so promptly after the sinking of the well was completed. She showed

114

interest and accepted a glass of water from the well, which she commended for its purity and taste. That was it. There was nothing to indicate how strenuous were the efforts of the Bangladesh Government to improve the conditions of life in outlying villages at this time, I can't imagine whom the film was designed to impress in 1988, because I remember the Jubilee Year of 1935 in Hooghly.

There were of course ceremonies to mark the Jubilee in Chinsurah, as it was the Divisional Headquarters, and as the Commissioner at the time (Rex Fawcus) had gone on to Burdwan for the occasion, I had to distribute the Jubilee Medals at a very select gathering on the Maidan (a Parade Ground). I also had to attend the opening of a village dispensary, for which I received a silver engraved trowel, which makes rather an unsatisfactory cake slice! For me it was a very hectic day which, after months when nothing seemed to happen apart from routine, was a very pleasant change, but it seemed to herald months of intense activity and publicity.

Within a few weeks I was told that I was being transferred to Calcutta as Excise Commissioner – and that meant finding accommodation in the City. I was pleased, therefore, when the Civil Surgeon suggested I accompany him to visit a colleague, one of the surgeons in Calcutta who had been in Chinsurah for some months, about some building

Raising water

115

problems in the local hospital. This would give me an excellent opportunity for contacting estate agents. The discussions were brief but satisfactory, as was the lunch that followed, and then one Civil Surgeon asked his colleague to have a look at a finger of mine which was somewhat swollen, though not very painful. 'The nail will have to come off, and the sooner the better,' was the opinion. He was preparing to take me off to the General Hospital straight away, when he remembered the gin and tonics that he had had before lunch. So I had the afternoon free for flat-hunting and, in the evening, went to Miss Riordan's Nursing Home for the nail operation, where I would spend the night. Before the operation I was asked if my presence at the discussion on the hospital problem was not a ruse to get me to Calcutta so that I had no choice but to consent to have the nail off.

Next morning I was still feeling rather groggy, but managed to scribble a few lines to my wife (who was in Shillong with a friend) to say I was OK, and got the car boy to drive me back to Hooghly. He looked after the car, but had taught himself to drive, and had a driving licence; so no law was being infringed. I could not have driven because I had a most conspicuous bandage on my left hand. (I have reason to mention this bandage. I do not refer to it merely as an embellishment!)

Serampore: Hindu-Moslem Riots

After reaching the house and looking forward to a restful day, I had just sat down to breakfast when the phone rang. When I lifted the receiver, a voice said, 'So, you are back in Hooghly. How did you manage to avoid all the police I had sent to intercept your car? Most of the police know the car.' It was the SDO Serampore speaking. I explained that I had not been driving, and he then told me there was Hindu/Moslem trouble brewing over an attempt to demolish a building which the Moslems claimed was a mosque. The Hindus said it was merely a hut. He would be glad of my presence. Like me, he was under orders of transfer, and the last thing either of us wanted was a Hindu/Moslem riot. For all the time I had been Magistrate at Hooghly-Chinsurah the two communities had lived peaceably together, and there had been no reports of latent animosity, which might flare up into open conflict, so the SDO's information was both unexpected and alarming. I wrote a note to the office postponing any work I had fixed for that day, and set off for Serampore.

The crowd that was waiting for me was smaller than I had expected, and less clamorous, but there was no doubt of its determination to resist and to frustrate the demolition of the building, which they claimed as a mosque. Reinforcements, if required, could come at once when called and, on the previous day, the numbers of those protesting swelled alarmingly within minutes. Strangely, although he was present, the Mohammedan who had had possession of the land on which the building stood, did not take the lead in giving reasons for objecting to the action that had been taken by the Hindu landlord, who had acquired legal possession of the property. He too was present, but he kept well in the background.

It took some time to discover the facts. The land had been leased by the Hindu landlord to a Mohammedan tenant, and when arrears of rent had accumulated for over three years, a suit was filed in the Civil Courts for their recovery and, in due course, a decree was passed. At this stage the tenant, instead of paying up, was ill-advised by lawyers and filed an appeal against that order in the Courts which, of course, he lost. Once entangled in litigation he could not stop. He must have paid more in lawyers' fees than the total of the defaulted rent. Against his objections the Court ordered the sale of the tenancy. This was brought in by the landlord, who then applied for delivery of possession from the Courts which, inevitably, was granted in spite of last minute objections by the tenant. Formal delivery of possession was given by an officer of the Court and a notice was posted.

As the land was near the centre of Serampore, and ripe for development a few days after delivery of possession, the landlord/owner sent his men to demolish the building, which stood in the middle of the plot. There was nearly a riot until the police were called and, to save trouble, they ordered postponement of the demolition, as their numbers were too few to cope with the mob. In spite of the vehemence of the claim that the building was a mosque, the landlord said that he had no knowledge of it being used for this purpose, and throughout all the various stages of the litigation, nothing had been mentioned about the religious character of the building. Only when the men went in for the demolition was the cry heard that this was a House of God, and in danger from a Hindu.

Certified Copies of the Orders of the Courts during the litigation over this land were produced, and none of them made any reference to a mosque, from which it could be inferred that at no stage was this plea raised. I then called for the Settlement Map and Record of the Area which, by law, was supposed to be a true representation of all the interests in the lands of the area. It had been prepared only a few years previously, and there could have been little change. Not only was there no mosque shown on the map, but there was no mention of any building, and all the officers in charge of the Settlement Work were most particular about noting any edifice used for religious worship and prayers.

Such damaging lack of evidence to support the plea that was now being urged was rejected by the leaders of the crowds. They said there was a mosque – and would listen to nothing to the contrary. They asked me to inspect the site, which was a most injudicious request for them to make, because when I went there I could see no resemblance to a mosque in the small brick structure in the middle of the plot. It consisted of just one oblong room, with a door and two windows. There was no path leading from the gate by the street to the door of the building and, obviously if it had been used, a pathway would have been necessary. There was not even any indication of the grass being trampled on.

I let it be known that the landlords were in the right, and were entitled to use the land of the plot in any way that suited them, and that included pulling down the hut. There was the cry that this was a mosque, and they would protect it. Then someone asked if this were not a mosque where would the local Moslems answer the call to prayer? Though this was not a very convincing complaint, I thought that, if there were a vacant plot of land somewhere in the neighbourhood which could accommodate a small mosque, the ordinary supporters who had been misled by the agitators would be satisfied. However, it was difficult to find even the smallest plot that was not covered with bricks and mortar. At last I noticed a little triangular piece of land which was part of the Government Estate, and therefore could be loaned by me, and I suggested that it would be made available for the erection of a mosque. It was not ideal, but I told them they should consider this very carefully.

By this time it was nearly 5.00, and I really had to leave. My finger had to have attention, and I did hope the leaders would, after what had been said that day, become more amenable to reason – and less aggressive.

I had a lazy weekend, and looked forward to going flat-hunting in Calcutta on the Monday, which was a Government Holiday for a Hindu Festival. To help me, the Deputy Secretary and his wife had asked me to lunch and, as I intended to call at Serampore on my way and might have had to spend an hour or so there, I packed a change for Calcutta.

Before setting out I phoned the Superintendent of Police, but the news was not what I had hoped for. The Fiery Crescent had been sent around, and there was increasing excitement and anger amongst the Moslems at the prospect of a mosque being pulled down. So great was the animosity that he had requisitioned additional Police, as well as some armed Police, to be sent to Serampore.

When I arrived there I found the Moslems more restrained than they had been some days previously, but equally more determined. There was, however, a significant change in their stance on the status of the building. They might insist to their followers that it was a mosque but, to establish that it had served a religious purpose, they provided a copy of the Koran which, they said, had been kept there. They could hardly have believed that such a wide cover could be given to buildings owned by Moslems nor that it would be acceptable in law. When told that the building had to be pulled down, they asked for time for consultation until 11.30. At 11.30 they again procrastinated and set 12.30 as the hour of decision. But by 12.30 most of the stalwarts, and others, wanted a meal, and the decision was again postponed until the afternoon. I had to phone my prospective hosts in Calcutta and explain that I could not leave Serampore while this potential trouble was simmering.

At 2.30 I was told to wait another hour, and then a request was made that nothing be done until 5.30, when the mills would finish for the day and release a band of Moslem workers eager for a fight. They were from Upper India, with no local connections, and were fine brawny specimens who could be guaranteed to stiffen any aggression by less militant Bengalis. There was danger of a serious riot, should these men come on the scene, so I gave the order that the demolition could be started. The Hindu landlord was called, and signed his request for the work to be started, but his hand shook as he was writing. Labourers had to be collected, so that half an hour elapsed before the first brick was removed from the building. Meanwhile a hostile crowd had been gathering, but remained passive as the police were seen to be in readiness for any violence. As soon as the demolition was begun, there was a battery of bricks as the police moved forward, but there were no casualties – only one constable who lost his pugaree! Most of the people contented themselves with cusses and empty threats. After about ten minutes the rain of bricks had ceased, though the shouting continued. After fifteen minutes all danger had passed in spite of growls of hate. At 4.30 I told the SDO, who had been with us all the time, that he could now go and get ready for his farewell party, which was given in the courtyard of the Sub-Divisional Office, once the headquarters of the Danish East India Company, and with the Danish Arms still above the entrance.

The Superintendent of Police and I made a tour round all the trouble spots and found that peace prevailed. Thus assured, we could seriously think of tea and gatecrash the SDO farewell party. We had had neither meat nor drink since breakfast, and the waiting game had been exhausting. Our entry to the party was more like an episode in a film than an incident in the administration of British India between the wars. The SDO was a Bengali member of the ICS and had proved both capable and popular, so there was a great turnout of the local *bhodralok* (gentlemen) to do him honour. There were some landlords, some barristers, as well as members of the Serampore Bar, and businessmen from Calcutta who still retained a connection with Serampore. As it was a Public Holiday and one of the hottest days in May, most of the guests, including the SDO who was himself a barrister, had elected to attend in the Bengali style of dhoti and white shirt.

Into this group entered two rather grubby British Officers in shorts, sweat-stained shirts, and carrying revolvers – the policeman's was in his gun holster and mine only too obvious in the pocket of my shorts. We were made welcome, for our presence confirmed that there was to be no riot. I forgot to mention that, as Serampore is not a large town, the centre of the trouble was barely a hundred yards from the scene of the party, and the guests were well posted as to what had taken place.

There was a brittle air of relieved tension about the proceedings, unusual in all the farewell parties that I have attended, and they have been many. There was little conversation and such as there was avoided the events of the day. The inevitable phoo-phoo band played with exceptional verve, 'It's a long long way to Tipperary' being taken at breakneck speed. After an hour or so the SP and I made another detailed tour of the troubled area, and found all was quiet, though the few pedestrians we met muttered insults under their breath. Satisfied with the situation, we decided that the time had come to leave.

As I approached my car one of the guests whom I had occasionally seen at gatherings in Serampore came up and introduced himself as a representative of Reuters. He said he had been impressed at the way we had handled what might have developed into a riot, especially as the legal rights of a citizen, as determined in a Court of Law, had been upheld. He promised that he would ensure that a full and appreciative account of the day's events would appear in the next day's *Statesman*. However, since there had been so little resistance, I wondered whether this would cause the Moslems to feel aggrieved, and perpetuate animosity between the two communities. No action was being taken against the men who had thrown bricks at the Police, and this I thought might help to allay any ill feelings that remained. In the end, he agreed not to write as he had intended, and I believe I acted wisely

Three days later I was again in Calcutta on the hunt for a flat to be ready when my wife came down from Shillong in about three weeks. The agent had just started up his car when I noticed a newsvendor's bill poster for the *Star of India*, with the words 'Police Fire at Serampore'. I had passed through Serampore half an hour previously, and there was no excitement. The police were not in evidence at all. I stopped the car in the traffic and bought a paper. The Moslems were not prepared to forget, as I had hoped. The report alleged that over the demolition of the building there had been some resistance, and the police had opened fire, with casualties among the crowd. No numbers were given, but it was hinted that they were numerous. There was a suggestion that the District Magistrate had received an injury (someone must have seen my spectacular bandaged finger and drawn the wrong conclusions).

As there was this report of firing by the police, I had to write a long statement to government explaining in detail what had happened. I had also to inform the Editor of the *Star of India* that there had been an incident but that the police did not open fire nor were there any casualties. I was making preparations for handing over charge and packing up, and was annoyed that much precious time had to be spent denying something that never happened. The Editor of the *Star* did not apologise for the incorrect report, and gave an explanation of such complete naiveté that it provided the Indian papers like the *Amrita Bazaar Patrika* with an excuse for much satirical comment on the methods of the *Star*, though they themselves were not averse to manipulation of the truth from time to time. It was said that, on receiving a hint that there was trouble in Serampore, a reporter had ben sent to investigate. Before he arrived at the outskirts of the town where the jute mills were, he had heard two stories about what had happened. One, much more alarmist than the other, alleged that two persons had been killed by the police firing, there were numerous serious casualties, and the District Magistrate had been wounded. Without going to the centre of the town or contacting anyone in authority he had returned to Calcutta with these two reports and the Editor, without further deliberation, thought it would be safe enough to print.

121

ON THE EVE OF THE DEPARTURE OF MR. D. MACPHERSON, I.C.S.

DISTRICT OFFICER, HOOGHLY

A TRIBUTE OF LOVE AND ESTEEM

Days are passing with change in their train,
Only a memory – and nothing else remain.
None is remembered, none is sought,
Amidst the oblivion everything lost.
Lo! the fortunates though are few,
Do in our memory live anew.
Master! you've been a champion of our cause,
And so we have never got to pause.
Calmly and boldly you fought and won,
Pressed out points on many a turn.
Having thus rendered your services here,
Everlasting a fame you so acquire.
Raised to the status of 'Excise Commissioner',
So you're going to have an hon'ble career,
Onwards you march to the path of progress,
Never-failing ever giving distressed redress.

Chinsura   **Officers and Staff**
The 10th June '35   *Of the Sadar Registration Office, Hooghly*

Shortly afterwards I was honoured with a farewell party – a more stolid affair than the SDO's – and, when it was over, the man from Reuters came to me and said: 'You see, I was right. All this bother came from influencing the Press. You meant well, but the Press knows best and with these people one can never win.' I believe that report in the *Star of India* was the beginning of the prejudice, which was believed in some circles, that I was anti-Moslem.

1935-1942: Commissioner of Excise, Bengal

For seven years from 1935 I was Commissioner of Excise for Bengal, an unusually long term for anyone in the Service to be in any one post. It began with the sensational discovery of an unlicensed distillery in the heart of one of the best residential parts of Calcutta. A fortnight after the trial of the principal accused, and his conviction and sentencing. I left for Jalpaiguri as Commissioner of the Division there.

For the first year and a half I was also Commissioner for the Salt Revenues. The Salt Tax was a Preserve of the Government of India, and the continuation of the two functions was a relic of the days when the British Power in India was almost confined to Bengal. In the run up to a Federal System of Government (which was never to materialize), the Board of Revenues at Delhi decided that the functions of Salt and Excise should be separated. It was a decision which may have been justified legally, but it was not very practical. I regretted it too because it reduced my reasons for requisitioning a launch to tour the Sunderbuns for an inspection of the Salt Works.

I always thought the Government of India did not acknowledge the value of my suggestion for the demarcation of the area in which the locally manufactured salt could be sold without tax, and without interference from Excise Offices. This happened before the Government of India decided against continuing the delegation of the enforcement of the Salt Tax Laws to the Government of Bengal. Agitation against the Laws was most extreme in Bombay when Gandhi assumed a leading role, but agitation can be infectious and soon there was very little salt manufactured in the villages near the Bay of Bengal. Moreover, such salt as was made, being coarse and not very white, was not acceptable in the markets only a short way inland.

As Collector and District Magistrate I had been in nominal control of the Excise work in my area. However, as there were so many other things which seemed much more important and urgent, like many other Civilian Magistrates I had left the running of the Excise Department to the Superintendent. I signed the papers he put up to me for signature with the merest minimum of scrutiny or understanding. Some were of amazing complexity in their attempt to be comprehensive.

I soon got the hang of the routine of the administration: the tests for Spirits and the control of Drugs – opium and ganja (now more popularly known as marijuana). Out there I found that, in a way which was not possible in the General District Administration, I was the Head and Leader of the Excise men, from the Superintendents down to the peons. As such, I came into very close contact with them in their work and got to know them as individuals. They came to see me more frequently for advice on personal matters as well as for guidance in their duties than the Subordinate Magistrates did in their approach to the District Magistrates. Illicit distillation was very prevalent because the Bengal Government with Moslem sympathies was pursuing a policy aimed at eventual Prohibition and the banning of dangerous drugs. In tackling these problems, they often had to act on their own responsibility, and were anxious for support and approval. Possibly the complicated nature of the prolonged investigation into the Whisky Fraud Case after the discovery of the illicit distillery made them appreciate the importance of working as a team, and a team must have a leader. They all, Hindus and Moslems, worked together without friction or animosity. Only when vacancies occurred did the latent hostility between the two communities prove troublesome. I was often thought to be anti-Moslem but, when I left, I think it could safely be said that no Moslem Excise Officer holding any position of responsibility had been appointed to this post for any reason other than his capability, and not for communal grounds. And that could not always be said. I believe what I had done was appreciated by both Hindus and Moslems alike.

I did write about some of my problems over these very tricky matters in my note to the India Office Records, and do not need to repeat them here.

Weddings, Funerals and a Film
One feature of these years which surprises me now to recollect was the number of Indian weddings which I was invited to attend – more than at any other time during my Service. I did not go to the religious ceremony, but to the reception, where only a brief call was expected after introduction to the young couple. I was pleased that these Superintendents and Inspectors should want me to be present when one of their children was married. I kept aloof from the formal

Addressed to

𝕯 𝔐𝔞𝔠𝔓𝔥𝔢𝔯𝔰𝔬𝔫, 𝔈𝔰𝔮𝔯, 𝕵.𝕮.𝕾.

Commissioner of Excise, Bengal.

Oh Reverend MacPherson Donald!
In thy possession – a heart very kind.
My commissioner! my superior Head!
Thou possessest a very pure mind.

A man of knowledge, a powerful man.
Having deep knowledge, thou a powerful man.

The most divine character I find
In thee, no pride in thy mind
I find. Horizontal lines of learning recede
Farther and farther as we proceed.
This spirit of University you attain,
And apply in life, and no vanity you maintain.
Even a poor peon can approach thy Honour.
Give thy patient ears and prescribe remedies thy Honour.

Thou possessest a very dutiful mind
Like that of the "Stern daughter of the Voice of God"

Long have been in our midst
We pray to God to see thee ever in our midst.
"Climb, climb up to the highest mount of glory"
Pray thy Honour to keep this servant in thy memory.

Submitted.
B.C.Das
2-5-42
At 10 A.M.
(on my way to office)

A presentation certificate

ceremonies – I thought they preferred it that way – except on two occasions.

In the first, a funeral, the family was not orthodox by any means, and yet not wholly Christian. The ceremony was more like a Christian ceremony, except that I did not attend the cremation. When he was ill the young officer had asked that I come to see him, and he had talked to me about the social works he and his sisters had been doing – without any thought at that time of dying. Naturally, when he died shortly afterwards, his sisters invited me to the funeral. This was the only occasion when I was formally asked to a funeral.

One afternoon a few months later I heard that another officer had died very suddenly. The following morning at 7.00, one of the Inspectors came to our flat and told me that the man's family said that the bier could not leave until I came to the house to give a last greeting. I hastily dressed and was driven to the house near Kalighat. I stood by the dead man and, in silence, placed my hand on his forehead in farewell. That was all. Then the bier was lifted and carried off to the burning ghat. I stayed for a few minutes to speak to his widow, and then left for the flat. I felt very humble that my presence should have been wanted at all. I have never spoken of it to anyone. I have always thought of it as a most private matter which I should keep to myself. And now I have recalled it on paper. I cannot bring myself to speak of it.

There were always unexpected tasks to be done, and one of the more unusual was to provide a script for a film on the Evils of Drink – to be called 'Saitan'. It was to be distributed free for exhibition as an extra slot in the local cinemas. The Director was to be a Bengali whose work had been highly praised by the critics in London, where his film on the Life of Buddha had a short run, not confined I believe to the specialist screens. The Government at the time, being mostly Moslem, hoped by this means to encourage a popular demand for at least a modified form of Prohibition.

Some of the senior Excise Officers wanted a scenario of drink leading to murder, with abundant gore. However, as that seemed out of what I thought would be the Director's style, I arranged for something much less melodramatic, and decided on a simple story of a village potter taking to the booze and so neglecting his work that he became a beggar, losing wife and home and children. I thought the jars and pots would be most picturesque, and the Director would have the opportunity of introducing scenes of village life, about which he was known to have been keen. I was prevented by a chill from being present when the film had its official presentation so cannot say what the general reaction was. I saw it some months later and was greatly impressed by the treatment. There was no exaggeration of the ruin that can come from drink when it has enslaved a man, and the ruins of the Bengal village were beautiful and most sympathetic. I doubt, however, whether any film intended as propaganda against drink could be effective. All the liquor shops were licensed by Government (the revenue was quite considerable) and, generally, the harm came from the illicit spirits, or local brews, which were crude, potent and often adulterated. A film about illicit distillation would have been more interesting, but it might not serve the purpose for which it would be intended.

1944: Jalpaiguri: Wavell's Visit

The absence of a telephone network in many districts of Eastern Bengal as late as the last War may surprise many users of British Telecom today, but I never could understand why large areas of Jalpaiguri were thus cut off from the outside world. The Commissioner's House was not half a mile to the west of the Teesta River and, while I could put a call through to all the District Headquarters in the Division, and to Calcutta, and probably also to London, I could not make contact with the Manager of a tea garden which was only ten miles distant, if it lay to the east of the Teesta. In emergencies one had to rely on messengers. On occasion, however, lack of the telephone could be advantageous.

Shortly after he arrived in Bengal as HE The Governor, the Australian Mr Casey had a small party in Darjeeling. Before it broke up the Military Secretary called me aside and asked me to arrange an opportunity for the Viceroy, Lord Wavell, to meet a number of the tea planters so that he could publicly acknowledge his appreciation of the work they had done in keeping open and strengthening the road to Burma for the passage of troops in convoy and of heavy military equipment and transport. A lunch was suggested with, as I was glad to learn, strictly limited numbers. All arrangements were to be extremely hush-hush. Lord Wavell intended to visit Sir Basil Gould, the Resident in Sikkim and an old friend. After that, he would go on to Assam (where the Japs were pressing on at Kohima) to visit his son who had been wounded and was in hospital.

These arrangements presented no problems. The only worry was whether the road from the airfield at Bagdogra, little more than an airstrip then, to Sikkim would be feasible on the date suggested for the trip. If the temporary 'cold-weather bridge' over a minor stream held, all would be well, but some four days before his arrival there was a sudden storm with torrential rain in the hills, and the stream became a raging torrent. The bridge was swept away and the stream was quite impassable. However, it subsided somewhat and, if the forest elephants were brought in, it could be forded.

Meantime I was receiving three or four coded messages per day giving me the times in the morning when the Viceroy's plane would touch down. Sometimes it would be 10.00 a.m., then 11.00 a.m., then 10.30 a.m. or 11.20 a.m., and I had to be at the airstrip to meet him. Owing to the uncertainty of the timing I arranged with a planter near Bagdogra to spend the night at his garden, so that I should be sure not to be late. So on the day before he was due to arrive I set out in the early afternoon. There had been only one code message that day, and this seemed to be the last and final one.

I had hoped that I might be able to cross the swollen stream further down but, when the car stopped halfway in mid-stream, I thought I could not risk going on. As I heard tigers in the forests I retreated, and threw myself on the hospitality of another planter, the Chairman of the Association. On the way, however, I stopped at a Police Station and explained how I had been prevented from reaching my destination, and wrote a note which the Sub-Inspector said he would have delivered to my original host.

In the morning I drove to the crossing where the bridge had been, and found an elephant waiting to take me to the east bank. Strangely for so small and narrow a stream in these exceptional conditions, it was very deep and the elephant could hardly keep its feet on the river bed. So I was able to meet Lord Wavell when his plane touched down exactly to the minute of the time on that last coded message. Wavell was in a hurry but, as there had been this heavy rainfall, the road was muddy and speeding was impossible. After seeing him and his party mounted on the elephants and crossing the rushing stream, I went to apologise to the planter who was to have been my host the previous night. When I did not turn up, he had realized what had prevented me and did not expect an explanation or apology. He got one, however. He was awakened at about 2.00 a.m. with a thunderous knocking at the verandah door. It was the constable with the message I had scribbled at the Police Station. I never dreamed that the man's journey would take nearly eight hours. He must have been very weary at the end of it, but he showed a spirit and determination which were not generally recognized amongst the country police force.

Back in the house at Jalpaiguri I was presented with another coded telegram. It had come just half an hour after I had set out the previous afternoon, but there was no one to get in touch with me, and I could not be recalled by a telephone message to a garden near which I would be passing. Everyone was so very sorry. They need not have been. Had I received the wire, I would never have been at Bagdogra to meet Wavell. It gave the definite final time for the touchdown exactly one hour earlier than the previous message – the actual time of arrival. There was no shade at the airfield then, and it was May with rising temperatures, so I would not have been prepared to wait in the sun for an hour.

In due course, the lunch given for the two Planters' Associations – Darjeeling and the Dooars – was a great success. Wavell did praise the effort made by the planters on the Burma Road, especially at the approaches to the fighting near Kohima, and spoke most highly about the loyalty of the coolies to their Managers, or most likely their Assistant Managers. Certainly their trust in the Managers in those dangerous conditions was a tribute to the understanding of the Managers, which they fully deserved. There was, however, one disappointment. After all the eulogy Wavell went on to say that, in the relaxed atmosphere of Gangtok, he had given much thought to the problem and had decided, as he thought everyone present would have heard that morning, to release Gandhi. But it was news to everyone at the table, and was very coolly received.

1944: Chinsurah

My last transfer was to Chinsurah as Commissioner of Hooghly and Burdwan Division. It was a transfer I never asked for, a transfer I never wanted and one which I tried to avoid. It meant that I had to forego a trek to the Jalap-La with the family, to which I had looked forward on my transfer to Jalpaiguri, and it would have been a memorable trip for Janet and Stella (my daughters) and one that they would never forget.

I had not sought the posting and when I received the transfer orders I had protested, but was told they had to stand. The officer I was to relieve had come into disfavour, because he did not press on with work for war supplies, and I had to take his place. Also, I was told that I had to go because there was anxiety over coal supplies, and the two principal officials in the area where the Bengal Coalfields were could not work

in harmony. As I was the only senior official who had any experience
of the mines, I was the inevitable choice to relieve the Commissioner
of the Burdwan Division who, according to the Coal Supremo,
frustrated all his efforts.

I was familiar with the area, and had retained friendly relationships
with many of the important Indians. I could not urge on Government
the real grounds of my reluctance, which were my wife's dread of the
house we should have to occupy.

Apart from the harassment and expense of a transfer, there were
many sad memories of the Commissioner's House in Chinsurah, which
would be with us all the time we were there, and my wife Marie felt
that there was an evil influence in the house which could affect the
lives of those who dwelt there. It was a house of unhappiness. There
were some, chiefly male, who escaped its contact but, when we arrived,
we were greeted by my predecessor's wife saying that her marriage
had broken up. And there were others of our predecessors whose tenure

Chinsurah, with family

of the post had brought them illness, bereavement and misfortune.

We had known it some years before, and it had sad associations for my wife. She thought of it as a house that could not bear happiness, and could only bring sorrow to those who had to live there. Men did not feel these pressures, but wives of some of my predecessors in the post had told her they had been glad when their husbands were transferred, and they could escape the brooding atmosphere of the house.

Architecturally, it was probably the most distinguished official residence other than the Colonial Palaces reserved for the use of the Viceroy and the Governor. It had been built at the beginning of the eighteenth century by the Dutch, and stood in a large garden on the banks of the Ganges, at a distance from the quarters of the other officials, and away from the hurly burly of the Indian town. Like many houses of the period, it had been designed for ostentation, with magnificent rooms to serve for official entertainments and receptions, but with scanty private accommodation. Two massive stairs with heavy balustrades under a lofty ceiling curved upwards to a wide landing, where one could picture the Dutch Governor and his Lady standing to receive their guests before they were ushered into the great drawing room, the men in their coats of brocade and the ladies in their paniered gowns. The effect was theatrical, impressive, and even welcoming, but in the rooms beyond there was coldness.

When these days of greatness had gone, the house had been robbed of some of its most notable fittings, and this was resented. Perhaps

Town school sports

131

dark deeds had been committed within its walls, and the Miagha lingered on. It was whispered that murder had been done, though never brought to justice. In the way that Claudius had contrived the death of Hamlet's father, an ambitious woman had rid herself of one husband, or it may be two. Her ponderous tomb was to be seen in the old cemetery two miles out of the town. In the church was a memorial to a Commissioner, his wife and his sister-in-law, who had died in the house within a few days of each other, and misfortune or bereavement had come to some of my acquaintances during their term of office in this post. Death has been a visitor to many houses, but seldom has it left so strong a sense of fatality.

I remember Lady Hogg, whose husband later acted as Governor of Assam, saying she was never so glad as when she heard that her husband was being transferred, because all the time she was there she had felt a sense of some weight bearing down upon her. Though I did not share these fears myself, I was never completely at ease. When Haldar met me for the formal making-over change, he was all too obviously suffering from a heavy night with the bottle. It was altogether a most inauspicious welcome to my new job. The expenses of the move made it even more of a financial burden than most transfers because we had to travel in the style of a past age, with a host of servants and animals. There was myself and my wife – the children came down from the Hills a month afterwards. We had a bearer, a *masalchi*, a cook with two wives and a youngster, a cat with kittens, a cow, poultry (I forget how many hens we had) and a young deer. No matter how carefully

Daughter Stella on merry-go-round, with ayah

the furniture was packed, fly-shunting, which was banned by the Railway (though, as we could hear from the house at Chinsurah, was being systematically practised at Naihati on the East Bank of the Ganges) wrought such havoc to chairs, tables and *almirahs* (wardrobes) that it required a month's solid work of a carpenter to patch them up.

Our arrival was inauspicious. We crossed the Ganges in a small boat. There were lowering skies when we set out, but halfway over a sudden squall blew up and, in the pouring rain, the boatmen feared we should not reach the other side. We landed at a ghat where a memorial had been erected to a Director of Education who had been drowned near that spot in similar circumstances.

Shaken as we were by this experience, we were greeted by my predecessor, bleary-eyed and barely recovered from a drinking session of the previous night. He showed himself only too anxious to depart as quickly as he could, and his manner was as curt as was possible without downright discourtesy. A more depressing welcome could not be imagined. Then his wife called mine aside to say that she hoped our time in the house would be happier than hers. It was a house of ill-luck, she said. It had brought her nothing but tears. She had come to the end of her tether. She had lost her only grandchild and had at last resolved to separate from her husband which, for an Indian lady, was the ultimate humiliation.

Such a reception did nothing to allay my wife's forebodings, especially as everywhere there was an atmosphere of neglect, not merely in the house but also in the surroundings. The garden was a wilderness, and the wide maidan towards the town was bleak and deserted. The Club, the common meeting place of the officials after a day's work, had been closed some years previously, and grass sprouted from the cracks in the cement of the tennis court. It was as if the effort to maintain morale had been lost, never to be recovered.

We carried on as best we could despite repeated illness and an ever-present depression. It was a struggle. Then one day in May something very peculiar occurred. Everything seemed to have lost meaning, to be purposeless, futile and exasperating. The rains had not broken, the sun blazed down relentlessly, and the air was still and threatening. The heat from which there was no escape, even under the fans, was stifling. Tempers were on edge, and nerves at breaking point. Breakfast had been late and burned, which was a disaster as supplies were strictly rationed. I was unduly testy with the servants, and regretted my hastiness. A bad beginning to a morning is seldom recovered during the day. I was given no chance to regain my lost composure. Work was interrupted by persistent and quite pointless phone calls; the files were intricate and badly noted, and I let my annoyance be seen only too clearly, for which I reproached myself. My wife too had felt the strain, and lunch was eaten in a grim and total silence. As soon as it was over, I left abruptly for my private office, which was located in the house, while my wife went upstairs without a word.

If anything, the reports were more frustrating than those I had had to deal with in the morning. I could not concentrate. I tried to focus my attention on the papers in front of me, but my eyes kept wandering to gaze at the slow-moving river and the mills beyond, which I could see through the open French windows. I thought of abandoning all pretence of work, when I was astonished to hear a voice coming, as it seemed, from the hall. It was calling my wife by name – 'Marie, Marie' – just those two words, and no more. It was a low-pitched woman's voice. It was a voice I knew, but when or where I had heard it I could not recollect. However, I was certain that whoever was there could not be the wife of any of the officers in the station.

It was an unusual time for any woman to call as it was mid-afternoon in the hottest month of the year, and then I remembered that there were no orderlies on duty at the entrance who might have helped her, though she must have known my wife very well. One orderly had been sent to the railway station two miles away to collect a parcel, and the other had taken a bundle of letters to the main office for despatch. So, in case the visitor was waiting for a reply, I went out to show her the way or to take her upstairs to my wife, who was probably resting in one of the bedrooms. But, to my amazement, there was nobody there.

I glanced round, and saw my wife standing on the landing. 'Did you hear anything?' she asked. I told her I had heard her name being called and had come out because the orderlies were away. She said she had heard the voice too, and wondered who it could be. She asked me to look in the garden and I went outside, but there was not a soul in sight. When I returned and told my wife this, she suggested that perhaps one of the servants might be wanting the *mali* (gardener), and we had misheard the call. She asked me to go down to the servants' quarters to find out. I thought this most unlikely, because the voice had not had a Bengali intonation, but I went down to the row of buildings where the servants lived. They were all shuttered against the heat and the burning sun. No one was stirring and the garden was deserted.

'There is nobody about,' I said and turned to go upstairs to join my wife. As I put my foot on the first step, almost at the place from which I imagined the call had come, I suddenly recognized the voice. I stopped, hesitated and went back to my office. Without a word, my wife re-entered the bedroom.

At the time I could not join my wife, as we should have had to talk over this strange experience, and I was afraid that I would upset her. I was disturbed in my mind, because the voice we had heard was that of a woman who had died in the house over ten years before, while we had been stationed in the vicinity. My wife had been fond of her, knowing that she was a true friend but she herself had not been happy, and the circumstances of her death had been unutterably sad and pitiful. The memory of those dark days had for years haunted my wife, and was the reason why she was averse to my being posted to this station. Had she a suspicion of what I suspected, she would have fled the house, believing it to be cursed.

Back at my desk I could not settle to any work. My thoughts were confused. Why had this happened? If I alone had heard the voice, I should have believed that I had dozed and it was part of a dream when half awake, or perhaps a hallucination. But my wife had also heard it, and she was in another room and at some distance from the hall. We could not both have been mistaken. Why had it happened? I could not think of any answer. It gave no message; it conveyed no warning; yet it left a feeling of unease, a feeling that something was wrong that should be put right, but without a hint of what it was.

Whatever the reason, I knew we had to remain where we were. I could not approach Government for a transfer on the grounds that my wife and I heard voices for which there was no accounting. That does not happen in the twentieth century. I decided, however, to avoid the subject in all talk with my wife. Fortunately, some acquaintances came in the evening and conversation turned to other topics, and the voice was never mentioned. Probably they would not have understood, but such matters are best kept private.

We stayed on for some more months, and had no other similar experiences but we lived in the house on sufferance, as it were. When eventually we departed, it was to leave India for good, though at the time we did not know it and had no intention that it should be our final farewell.

Asansol

It was some weeks after we arrived before I could go up to Asansol, the centre of the Bengal Minefield, and during that time I had no word from the Supremo. I heard that he had not been well, but the silence after all the fuss he had made to have Haldar removed prompted the suspicion that he had ceased to be bothered about the problem of coal. The PWD had begun the white-washing of the house, and bamboo scaffolding was in the main stairway when HE the Governor, Ian Casey of Australia, called in for tea in the course of one of his tours. We were still unpacking and could only use the lower verandah looking towards the river for his entertainment. He was much more patient than his chauffeur and guards, who insisted on instant refreshment and made the bearer very nervy. When, at last, I had to go to a meeting of a Coal Committee, Marie decided she would not stay in the house alone and would come with me, and she could not leave our Siamese cat Tibby behind.

That night I remember more clearly than anything that happened to Coal at midday. In all my many visits to Asansol I never noticed many cats around, but within hours of arrival at the bungalow, all the tom cats from miles around seemed to know that a queen had come amongst them, and they came flocking to the bungalow to offer their respects and love. They were very loud in their protestations. We had hardly one hour's sleep that night. Tibby, however, seemed quite unmoved by all this serenading, and remained curled up in the basket.

The Coal Committee Meeting was almost a non-event. The Supremo sent his apologies for absence – ill-health he said – and of the twenty members few had anything to say that was of any relevance. None of them showed any anxiety and nobody had a useful suggestion to make though the meeting lasted two hours, but there were no complaints, and that was something. I had the impression that the Coal Industry was getting back to normal – if it were not already functioning better than usual. However, it was unanimously decided that there should be another meeting before the year was out. After the talking was over, I heard of the general dissatisfaction with the Supremo, which made me more than ever annoyed at my transfer with all its attendant discomforts.

He had arrived in India with a great flourish, and set up an office, but intimated that he could not run it efficiently unless he had the services of his secretary who had been left behind in England. His wife had also been left behind. His manner rather annoyed the Mine Managers while he was surveying the situation before drafting a plan for improvement. However, he had the ear of the Government of India, which approved his demand for bringing his secretary out from

England. When she arrived, everybody realised she was in no condition to undertake any secretarial duties. Within a few weeks she had produced his son! During all this time the Supremo seemed to have been very worried, and anxious, though not about coal. It was shortly after this, and about the time of my arrival in Chinsurah, that he became ill and stopped attending to any work.

I can't remember if there was another Meeting. There may have been but, if there were, it would have been quite unnecessary, and the Government of India seemed to have realized this at last. The Supremo's contract was ended, and he had to return to England before the end of the year.

In the middle of December I had to attend a Conference of Commissioners in Calcutta and, as a matter of courtesy, I thought I might invite him to lunch before he left. This invitation and his reply constituted the only correspondence between us in the time since I had taken over in Chinsurah. He could not accept but asked me to have lunch with him at the United Services Club, as he could not spare the time from his packing. I went: it was a rather sad occasion. He was there with his secretary and the infant. We never spoke one word about coal. All he could talk about was the child, and I hope I did not falter in my admiration. He was a fine healthy specimen of a baby boy, and his father was quite besotted with him. It was really pathetic the way he spoke about the infant, and he was hurt that he was leaving the child behind in the East while he was returning to England the next day. I was sorry for the secretary, who was a very quiet sort of woman who had been brought out to India in a hurry for a position that never was, and would have to go to Ceylon with the child till the war was over. I never asked if she had friends there, or whether she could find work, but she seemed to accept her fate. He must have felt that his months in India had been a waste of time – for the coal industry had done for itself what he had come out to do.

The Government of India was so sure that the coal industry was back to normal that, within three months, it was devising schemes for welfare in the mines that could only be effective if there were trained staff to work them – and trained staff there were none. Hundreds would be needed.

Looking Back

Looking back, after a quarter of a century, on the years I spent in India, it is often the small incidents that most readily come to mind. Incidents of no importance, at times no more than a glimpse of an unheeded gesture but each, in its way, affording a vignette of one aspect of the people of the country. These few random recollections may be of interest. Some are amusing, some I should rather forget. What follows now is not a continuous narrative, but a succession of memories of isolated happenings which have struck me as being worth recall.

Our Servants

We never could have carried on our work if we did not have the servants, many more than we could have required in Britain, even prewar. And, in all sorts of ways, they were the Indians with whom we most came

Donald's bearer

139

into contact. Inevitably, there were probably more tales to be told about them than about any other class of people of the country, not all condescending.

In the offices it was traditional that the peons and orderlies (*chaprassis*) were men from up-country, chiefly Bihar and the United Provinces. Some might eventually settle in Bengal, but the majority would return to spend their old age in the villages where they had been born. On the domestic side of our existence in the country, Ooriyas from Orissa were ordinarily the bearers of the Magistrates and Collectors when I first went to India. Some years previously Bihar, with Orissa, had been joined into Bengal and, on account of their sporting opportunities, Bihar Districts were preferable to many of the rather dull Mofussal districts of Bengal, and young civilians were sent to learn their trade in Bihar. The first servants acquired by them when newly arrived from Britain would usually be Biharis. Once the separation of the two provinces was effective, more servants from Bengal, most frequently Mohammedans from Dacca, were taken on but, latterly, they were superseded by men from the Hills, Nepalese chiefly. They were so much more adaptable and cheerful. To begin with, all of them were most unsophisticated and unused to the ordinary customs and usages of modern life as practised by the British in India.

1920: One day I was very surprised when Father wrote in his letter that, much as the family enjoyed receiving my epistles, they would greatly appreciate not having to pay 'Postage Due' on them. That I could not understand. I gave the peon money for the stamps required every Thursday when I sent off my weekly mail, along with the letters from the Office. Thursday being Mail Day before regular Air Mails were set up, I reserved it for tackling outstanding correspondence as well as family mail, and there usually were some letters, as well as the regulars, from friends in the UK and also in India – to say nothing of bills that had to be paid. There was usually some change out of the notes I gave the peon (never new 1 Rupee notes though – usually very dirty and worn ones). I always assumed they were correct. I never checked them. To solve this problem, one Thursday I limited myself to only one letter – for the family. When I gave it to the young peon I gave him two and a half annas, which I told him was the exact cost of the stamp that would be needed. I reiterated that he should get a 2½ anna stamp. Half an hour later he returned. He looked very pleased with himself and he said, 'Sahib, you gave me too much money. I got the stamps for 1 anna [that was the denomination for Indian internal postage]. Here is the change of 1½ annas.' He was so proud of what he had done that I could hardly bring myself to tell him that he had done exactly what I wanted him not to do, and another 'Postage Due' would be delivered in Edinburgh. I am sure that, when the family knew the story of this stamp, they felt it was worth all that extra postage dues that they had paid.

1921: Sometimes the servants could prove an embarrassment and place one in a very false position. During Settlement, in order to secure a true record of the rent paid for each holding and the status attached to the tenancy, evidence was taken in the presence of representatives of both the landlord and of the tenants who actually tilled the land. It was Statute Law that, should there be no change in the rent paid by a tenant cultivator for twelve consecutive years or more, it should be presumed that the rent had been fixed in perpetuity. It was an issue in many places where the interests of the tenants and of the landlords clashed. As often as not the poor cultivator had not kept all the rent receipts needed to substantiate his claim, while the landlord's men would not produce the rent accounts. In one place, where the contests were keenest, the landlord's agent thought to bring the tenants to reason by attending the initial preparation of this record on an elephant.

An elephant can do massive damage to the rice crop on the small plots (one third of an acre) of the tenants and, as the Kamingo did not

Donald's driver

stop in one spot, but went from field to field while his agent and the cultivators went along with him, the elephant could roam around as well. A very high proportion of the crop was ruined. While some sympathy could be felt for a landlord obliged to abide by a fixed rent roll in years of rising prices, the employment of an elephant to obtain an increase of the rent could not be tolerated. I sent in a report of the incident to the District Magistrate in Patna, with evidence to substantiate the facts. The Agent was summoned to Court.

Shortly after that I was on tour in another part of the District where the landlord, whose agent had used the elephant, had property. Hearing of my arrival one of his men was sent to greet me with a most sumptuous *dali* – a gift of fruit, fowl and vegetables and, among the mangoes was hidden a bottle of Scotch. I was tempted to accept but, in the circumstances, with the Magistrate having summoned the agent, acceptance of so magnificent a *dali* was quite impossible. I made my reason for rejecting his gift perfectly clear. I ensured that the men who brought his gifts took them away and did not leave anything behind.

I had to leave the place in about an hour, but found the cook had gone to the bazaar and had not returned. As he was essential to my existence, I had to wait till he came back. I did think he had stayed away an unusually long time. I forgot to mention that, in this watery area with the monsoon approaching, I had to use country boats for travelling, and spend the nights on the split bamboo flooring. The portable mattress I bought on arrival in Bengal some years previously proved indispensable. Next day, and for the week that followed, I was grateful to the cook for the excellent 'shopping' he had done in the bazaar. He provided duck and specially fat chickens, such as were not usually available in the bazaars when on tour in the outlying areas of a Mofussal District. Then there was a quarrel amongst the staff.

I never heard what it was about, but it seems to have been bitter, because I was informed of the source of all that unusual food. After the landlord's servant had retired with all the *dali*, the cook and I think one or two others of the servants who accompanied me on tour, went to the landlord's office and probably intimated that I had changed my mind over the refusal. At any rate they asked for, and got, all the special edibles. As they said these had been obtained in the bazaar, they charged me what they thought was the market rate – and that was the maximum rate! I let them know that I was annoyed because they tainted my good name with the landlord's agent. At the time, however, there was nothing I could do so long as I was on tour but, back in Patna, I did give the cook notice. I also wrote a stiff letter to the agent and told him that he should have known me better than to believe that I would adopt such a devious manner to accept the *dali*. I explained that the servants acted without my knowledge and, finally, that I had had to pay them, as I understood that they had actually bought everything in the local market. I had not benefited in any way from his solicitude for my comfort.

On the other hand, in an emergency the servants usually exerted all their energies to ensure that the Master was not inconvenienced, embarrassed or 'let down' before his friends. One Christmas Day it was my turn to host the Regulation Dinner for Members of the Club and the Missionaries. All preparations had been made well in advance and carefully discussed with the cook, a man of the Hills. I was confident all would be well on the night when, in the morning, the cook told me there was something he had forgotten to get in the bazaar.

In the evening I went to the Club for a game of bridge, so that I would be out of the way when the final preparations for the table were in progress. At 7.00 a worried *chaprassi* arrived at the Club to inform me that the cook had just been brought back drunk, and completely insensible to everything. And the guests were coming at 8.00. None of the servants was kitchen-trained, but all were able to cook their daily curry and rice. They promised they would do their best and I could count on the dinner being up to standard for Christmas Day – but it might be late. I added nearly a bottle of sherry to the clear soup, and kept the short drinks on tap for rather longer than usual.

Nobody noticed, or cared, that a very late start was made with the soup – or that the remainder of the meal had been in the hands of amateurs. Everyone declared that everything had been done in style, and a good time had been had by all. The cook did not recover until the third day. On the second day he was so still that I was becoming anxious, and the servants thought he was going to die.

1922: There was, of course, a very strict recognition of rank amongst the servants, and none of the others would dare argue with the bearer, so it was with some trepidation that I heard a sweeper in one of the Dak Bungalows where I had to put up for the night swearing at the bearer and calling him the worst of names. The noise he made was ear-splitting. I was rather annoyed because I hadn't been given my morning tea in time, also I had found it unusually tasteless, so I called on him for an explanation of his wrath. What sort of servant is he, I was told, who cannot even make his Master tea correctly with boiling water. It seemed the sweeper always took the tea leaves after I had finished my tea and boiled them. That morning the water for my tea had not been boiling, and the sweeper found his tea quite undrinkable. I had poor service from the bearer for some time after that.

But sometimes sweepers may have been expected to give other services than those associated with the *ghusul khana* (bathroom) and the thunder-box (the commode). After the joint Settlement Camp in Barkina in the winter of 1919-20, as part of our training, we were sent out in pairs to write up the records for some villages. My companion was Tom Ellis, whose father was the Principal of a Non-Conformist Theological College. For our village we had to pitch our tent in a very open spot at some little distance from any homestead, so we asked the headman to arrange to send us a sweeper. 'Of course,' he replied, 'what do you want – a *chokra* or a *meyey manush*?', i.e. a boy or a girl? Both of us were surprised, and rather shocked that the headman had thought we would be anxious for a girl, and that he was quite ready to supply one. It never crossed our minds that the headman thought we might prefer a boy – or that a boy would be available. The year was 1920 not 1989. Perhaps the Indian equivalent of the *droit de seigneur* must have been prevalent there. The sweeper who was sent had grey hairs and his limbs were shaking.

Especially in the districts outside the big towns, which until recently lacked what are now considered the normal facilities for

Marie MacPherson with two bearers, one holding Donald's topee while he takes the photo

communication, one was dependent on the lowly paid *chaprassis* or messenger orderlies for passing on one's orders. They were in constant attendance at the office and at one's residence.

After I was married one of these, a white-haired old man with many years of service, showed unmistakably his opinion of women in general. I had had to go on tour and, when my wife called for the paper which was delivered at the house each morning, he told her that, as the Sahib was absent, he had sent it away. Newspapers, in his opinion, were for Men Only.

And there was the other one who, on returning to the house during the monsoons when the roads were deep in mud, went into the kitchen where I found he had just dried his feet on the dish cloth. 'Oh,' he

Tea on the lawn: Tom Ellis (Donald's best man); Marie MacPherson; Jean Watson-Bishop (Marie's aunt); Donald

said, 'it will be washed,' but he had placed it where it would be used for the teacups. Needless to say, he was sent to work solely in the office. With such indifference to ordinary health safeguards, can one wonder that sickness and disease were so prevalent?

Another orderly in that same district within a few days after I had joined, complained to me that a neighbour was harassing him, by encroaching on the plot where he was building a house. He asked for my personal intervention, and I was sympathetic until I visited the site and found that the neighbour was not in the wrong, and the house the orderly was erecting could not have cost him less than £400. This was in the years of the depression when that sum would buy a good solid house for a middle class man. As the man's pay was only £15 per annum, which might be considered less than a starvation wage, I wanted to know how he had found the money for such a substantial dwelling. He did not expect such a question and was transferred to duties where he would have fewer opportunities for supplementing his income.

It has to be recognised that, with the introduction and development of democratically elected representative governments in India, similar methods of improving their finances were adopted by persons of a much higher status. On one occasion a man who had been successful in obtaining a grant to run a shop for the sale of intoxicants, when asked to submit the required deposit for the grant of his licence, applied for time as he had no ready cash. He had paid away so much to obtain the influence of the Chief Minister, that he could not meet the small demand that was made. With the courage of desperation, he made a statement to me, which was put into writing, in which he detailed the amounts he had spent, the persons to whom these had been given, and the circumstances in which they had been demanded. The statement was kept for record.

I can also remember the agent of a landlord who had owned expensive properties in the coal-bearing districts at a time when there was competition for mining rights. He had become an Honorary Magistrate and lived in style on a salary of £150 per year. When he died, shortly after he had been dismissed by his master, who had been made aware of his activities, his estate was estimated by the lawyer applying for probate of his will at £100,000 and that, for obvious reasons, would not be an exaggeration.

The Miners
In the mining districts, housing for the workers was for the most part

very poor and inadequate, because much of the labour was seasonal, and the hutments were often vacated for months at a time, when the men would go to attend to their fields in their distant home villages at sowing time and at harvest. Maintenance was a problem, but the accommodation was of a meagre standard. When, over a few drinks, I commented on this to an Indian mine owner and said that many of the huts were little better than cattle sheds, he agreed, but added, 'Well, these people are just like cattle; what do they need, what can they expect?' He was a man of considerable wealth and influence, and a few days afterwards was to leave for Geneva at the insistence of the Government of India to attend a Conference on Labour Relations called by the United Nations within months of the cessation of hostilities in Europe. Doubtless, he did not voice these sentiments on the shores of Lake Leman, but I am convinced that this was an instance of *in vino veritas*. Nor was he exceptional. Generally the conditions for the labour force were worst where the management was Indian.

In spite of everything, the miners were an uncomplaining lot. Many were aboriginals who would have starved if they had had to subsist on the produce of their small holdings. They worked hard and, defying all propaganda from a prohibitionist intentioned Government, they persisted in a fondness for strong drink, a rice beer called *pachwain*. I met a crowd of them one afternoon. They were sitting in a circle, the pot of *pachwain* was circulating. For them it was early in the day and they were still sober. I asked them why they did not try to save their earnings and why they spent money in this way. 'Well,' said the leader, 'We feel we have deserved this. We work down the mines all week, and now we are free for a day or two to enjoy ourselves in the open air. We brew the *pachwain* [probably illegally]. We sit around and talk. We drink and laugh and sing. We do no harm to anyone. And, if we get drunk, we forget the existence we lead, and are "Kings for a Night". I can never forget the brave tone in which he said those words – 'We are "Kings for a Night".' There could be no answer. In their own way, they achieved some happiness.

Famine and Disease
The heavy toll that disease took on people in all classes, the prevalence of epidemics such as cholera and smallpox, and the high rate of mortality, were the causes of what often seemed callousness to the sufferings and the hardships of the less fortunate. The struggle for existence can breed an indifference which may appear shocking.

To

D. Macpherson Esq., I.C.S

Commissioner, Burdwan Division
ON THE OCCASION OF
Free Distribution of Cloths to the Poor
AND OPENING OF
Umesh Chandra Sen Gupta Memorial Hospital
AT MATO

SIR,

OUR hearts 'leap up when we behold' you in our midst. You are the refuge of the sick and destitute, the poor and helpless, you act as their 'Friend, Philosopher and Guide'. You talk to them, feel for them and elevate them from the abyss of oblivion. We are proud of your achievements and proud above all of your sincerest desire to come in close contact with 'the bold peasantry, their country's pride', who, 'when once destroyed, can never be supplied.'

VILLAGES are villages all the world over and this village like all villages, of our Thana, unaccustomed that it is to greet the Officers of Rank and Renown, is sanctified to-day by your presence. Glory to **Mr. Kali Charan Sen**, glory to his benevolent activities, which account for the presence of your exalted personality and pave the way for local prosperity.

MATO
P.S. Amta, Dt. Howrah.
17-11-45

Members
Amta Thana Union Board Association

A presentation certificate

During the famine of 1943, when thousands died of starvation, the Bengal Government opened the equivalent of soup kitchens in village centres throughout the country. The fare supplied was sufficient only to keep alive the spark of life in emaciated bodies. It was all that could be done. Supervision of these arrangements for feeding the hungry had to be left to the village elders or headmen. Many took on the work as a troublesome chore, and one old grey-beard asked, 'Why does the Government bother to feed all these old widows? They have done nothing for twenty years; they have husked a little rice. They have lived on charity. They would be better dead.' Perhaps a quick and painless death would have been a merciful release; but humanity could not stand by while wretched men and women slowly wasted away for lack of food.

There were many heart-rending scenes during that terrible year, but the one I remember most vividly, and the one I should be glad to forget, is of arriving at Siliguri at the foothills of the Himalayas to catch an afternoon train. The station was crowded with passengers moving from carriage to carriage to find a compartment to their liking. No one seemed to notice a bundle of rags lying at their feet in the middle of the platform. Nobody seemed to care, neither passengers nor station staff, that the man was dead. Nobody knew who he was, how he came there, nor where he had come from. He had lain down and died, and the mob of people milled round his body, intent on their own immediate affairs, without a thought for him. I called the Station Master, who called the sweepers to remove the corpse. They lifted it up, without anyone stopping to ask what they were doing, and then carried it to an outlying part of the station yard, poured paraffin over it and set it alight in full view of all who had had the good fortune to secure a seat in the train.

The Story of Three Lost Days.

In 1923 when elections had to be held for the new Legislative Assemblies in Bengal, members of the caste beyond the pale (the untouchables) were given the right to vote if they were of sufficient substance. However, they were to be called men of the Scheduled Castes.

Not all Indians were sympathetic and one *zamindar* (landowner) in Backerganj, a district in what is now Bangladesh, issued commands to all his tenants as to how they were to exercise their franchise. When he found out that some of them, and especially those of the Scheduled Castes, had shown an independent spirit, and voted contrary to his wishes, he told his agents to call these men to his local *katcherry* (local rent collection office) and make them aware of his annoyance.

The tenants took umbrage at the uncalled for reprimand, which was strongly worded and quite unreasonable. Angry words were exchanged and at last the agents, who were accustomed to docile compliance, acted as they had always done when they met with opposition, and used force to emphasise their displeasure. The tenants resisted and there was a scuffle, in which some of them received slight injuries, a minor cut and some bruises.

A few years previously they might have been resentful but would have accepted this treatment as an inescapable condition of their lowly lot. However, emboldened by their new status, they decided that the agents should learn that they were not above the law and that a complaint should be filed before the Magistrate. This was a sort of private prosecution much in use for all manner of petty village quarrels and disturbances. A medical certificate was obtained regarding the nature of the injuries and, armed with this corroboration, one of them who had the worst of the bruises, appeared before the Magistrate and made a sworn statement. After a few questions and a scrutiny of the medical certificate, the Magistrate issued a Summons on the agents who had been named to attend his Court and answer all allegations made against them.

It so happened that the Sub-Divisional Magistrate, who would normally have had to try the case, was himself a member of the Scheduled Castes, and as I was the Additional District Magistrate, he came to me for advice. His problem was that should he try the case and end up convicting them, allegations would be made that he could not be other than prejudiced. On the other hand, were he to acquit them no member of his community would believe that he had done so out of an honest assessment of the evidence that had been given. It would be assumed that he had been improperly influenced against giving the *subichar* (good justice) that was due. I appreciated his difficulty so, as my own file was not heavy at the time, and the alleged incident had arisen from this first democratic election, I agreed to hear the case, though it was not of the type I would normally have tried.

In due course both parties appeared. On one day I recorded the evidence for the prosecution, and on a later day the evidence for the accused. There was then cross-examination of the witnesses for both sides. That there had been an incident was not the issue. It was only whether the force used by the agents on the man could be construed as an assault.

The evidence in such cases is never very satisfactory or clear cut; the witnesses are illiterate, their testimony is taken weeks after the occurrence, and memories often have unconsidered lapses. Generally the parties settle out of court and honour is satisfied. Neither of these parties could withdraw without loss of face, and the proceedings dragged on for longer than I had anticipated. The Scheduled Caste witnesses for the Complainant were often hesitant. The effort of recollection seemed hard, but they gave the impression that they were telling what they did remember, and were more or less consistent in what they said. The witnesses for the agents were prompt in their replies, sometimes almost too prompt, and showed that they had been very well drilled in what they said they remembered of the quarrel. After the first of them had had his say, each man who followed repeated almost word for word the testimony of his predecessor at the witness stand. There seemed to be a recognised order for the questions asked in cross examination, and one of their men answered the question he had expected to be asked and not the question that he had actually been asked.

At last all the evidence was recorded and a day was fixed for hearing the arguments of the respective lawyers. It was the Wednesday of the following week. I remember it was a Wednesday because of what happened afterwards. Great store was put on these arguments. The lawyers always wanted time to study the records of the evidence and to prepare their addresses. Bengalis have a ready flow of eloquence on any subject and at any time, and these arguments are usually very lengthy and time-consuming and often not very relevant to the issue involved. However, the lengthier these addresses are, the better the clients seem to be pleased. For this reason, in expectation of hours of weary listening, I kept my file clear of other work for the day of the final hearing.

When I arrived in Court I could see the accused, their legal advisers and their friends, amongst whom I recognized several of the witnesses whom I had examined. They were talking together in a mood of what appeared to be confident high spirits, as if they knew they were assured of victory. The Scheduled Caste Complainant was absent, but a friend was there to say that he had gone to bring his lawyer. A little later he arrived to say that the lawyer could not be found, though he had searched every conceivable place where he could reasonably be. The man seemed dazed and bewildered and in obvious distress. The defendants and their lawyers showed unrestrained jubilation; they seemed to take for granted that there would be immediate judgment in their favour, and asserted that the failure of the opponent's lawyer to attend established the falsity of the charges brought against them. They claimed that the lawyer had thrown up his brief because he realized nothing he could say would help his client and then, with strange inconsistency, added that he had not come to Court because he had not been paid. This the Complainant most indignantly denied. He declared that he and his friends had been in town the previous day, and had paid their lawyer whatever fees had been asked, and had discussed with him points that he might find useful in his address. They just could not understand his absence. When they found he was not in Court shortly before the hour fixed for the hearing, they had gone to his place of business and then to his lodging in the town, but he was nowhere to be found. They begged for a short adjournment to the following day and said they would do all in their power to secure his attendance. I felt that their anxiety was genuine and that they were telling the truth.

Normally, if a lawyer were to give up his brief, especially at such a late stage in a case, he would have informed me of the fact. I thought it was out of character for this particular lawyer to have abandoned his clients without warning or explanation, when all the evidence had been taken, especially as he had been so diligent on their behalf at all stages of the hearing until then. I might have heard arguments from the lawyer of the other party, but decided to allow the adjournment, so that the justice might seem even-handed. The Complainant still pressed his charges.

Next day he had to report that the lawyer was still missing. He could not be contacted anywhere. He seemed to have vanished. Another adjournment was asked for and this I reluctantly granted. On the third day the Complainant had again to admit that he could not produce the lawyer. He said he had searched everywhere in the town for him and could not understand why he had deserted them after being paid. My clerk confirmed that the lawyer had not been seen in the vicinity of the Courts for several days, and this was very strange. The agents' lawyer pressed that he begin his address, but was so scathing and contemptuous of the Scheduled Caste men, who had dared to cause a Summons to be issued on a landowner's agents for a mere exchange of words, that he did not gain the sympathy for his clients that he had hoped for.

At last the Complainant said that if, after one final effort to get in touch with his lawyer in the town, he did not succeed, he would try to engage another firm from the local Bar and, should he have no luck there, he would go to Calcutta and bring an advocate to speak for him. It was Friday, and as a weekend would intervene, he might just be able to do so. It was a rash promise, if it were not sincere. There was no gainsaying his earnestness, and the determination and assurance of his friends of the Scheduled Caste. I felt I had to give them a chance, but it would be a last chance. I agreed to adjourn the case until the next week, but not later than Monday. No further time would be allowed. This was accepted by the Complainant and he promised faithfully to bring someone of the legal profession to speak for him.

On the Monday, when the case was called, a young advocate from Calcutta appeared for the Complainant. He was also of the Scheduled Caste and entered politics most successfully some years later, rising to be a Minister in one of the Coalition Governments during the war years. After all the vituperation and wrangling of the previous week, the proceedings on that final day were brief, tame and in fact something of an anti-climax. The lawyer from Calcutta said all that could be said from a study of the evidence as recorded. It was after all a simple case, and there was little basis for any elaborate arguments. The address for the agents was muted in tone, devoid of all the usual and expected rhetoric. It kept strictly to the facts, and displayed none of the indignation so marked in the earlier stages of the trial at the presumption of these low caste persons in bringing such allegations against their betters.

In the end I convicted the agents and imposed a small fine, such as would have been customary in similar village cases of a breach of the peace. There could be no appeal against such an order, but provision had been made in the Codes of Procedure for a reference to the High Court where there was an obvious miscarriage of justice. The High Court was approached, but refused to interfere.

Some months later, the Head of the Baptist Mission (and what more reliable informant could I have had) told me what had happened on those three lost days, and it showed how exaggerated was the trust that litigants had in these addresses by their lawyers. The lawyer for these tenants was not at the head of his profession in the town, but he was competent and conscientious and had a good practice. He was very lean, almost gaunt in appearance and, when in Court, was very shabby and careless in his dress. Many of his clients were poor and, as he always seemed considerate to them, I formed the opinion that he was a man of law with a social conscience. How mistaken I was! Much of what he earned was spent on wine and women and, at the time of the trial, he was paying regular calls on a certain apparently well known 'lady of the town' as she would then have been discreetly called.

She must have had unusual allure because, by the time I heard about her, she had become the central figure in a most sensational and, for the Bengali Officers of the District, a most scandalous murder case. The Head of Clerk of the Judicial Record Room had killed his rival for her favours – the Chief Court Inspector of Police, who attended to the Criminal Work before the Magistrates, and appeared as Prosecutor in many of the cases in their Courts. As might be expected, stories about her had a wide circulation!

By some means or other (but in India little of one's private life is secret from the gossips of the bazaar) the *zamindar*, his agents or perhaps some member of the local Bar had learned of the lawyer's nocturnal habits. They plotted with the woman to take advantage of his weakness to secure the collapse of the charges that had been brought, by preventing the lawyer from attending Court on what would have been the final day of the trial. The accused agents would be acquitted and the discomfiture of the Scheduled Caste tenants complete.

So it was arranged that, when he visited her on the night before he was to argue the case before me, she would make him very welcome, ply him with the country wine and add a potent sleeping mixture. The scheme worked. Next day, when he should have been in Court, he was lying in her room oblivious to everything in a dull doped stupor. The elation of the accused agents and their friends, which I noticed when I took my seat on the Bench, was understandable. As adjournments were granted she, apparently, was persuaded to continue her hospitality to the lawyer for the two successive nights. On the Friday he was still in her room in a sort of coma. She could not retain him in that condition over the long weekend which followed but, by that time, the agents had probably realized that all their scheming had miscarried.

The lawyer must have had the father and mother of a hangover on coming to life again. When he was able to appreciate what had happened, he was so ashamed that he retired to his family home in an out of the way village, and remained there for well over a month to regain his health and to try to forget. I did not see him about the courts for many weeks afterwards.

Often there seems so little to choose between the evidence given for the two opposing sides in a criminal Court that one may well wonder in retrospect whether one's decision had been justified. If I ever had any slight suspicion of a doubt that I had been mistaken in my judgment in this case, it would have been extinguished by this story of the unscrupulous trick that was intended to obtain a judicial victory over the Scheduled Caste tenants for an act of independence and so keep them down for years.

Shooting of Col. Simpson at Writer's Buildings
(from a letter to his sister, Betty, dated 8.12.30)

It will do me good to get a letter off my chest tonight. After today's happenings I have more than a bit of a head and, though I normally feel somnolent after dinner, I am as awake as if it were morning.

Perhaps there is nothing to tell. The papers will tell you most of the news, but I know you will wonder where I was at the time and what I heard. Writer's Buildings, where all the Local Government is, is on three stories, and the offices are arranged along a verandah with sundry passages leading to other offices which, perhaps because they are busier, do not receive hordes of visitors.

Each story has more or less the same layout. I was on the third story, and my office is one of the coolest in Calcutta. Well, today everything was going well. I had had a topping letter from the Collector of Burdwan about my engagement, and was looking forward to a pleasant evening with Marie. At about 12.30 I suddenly heard a crackle, then another and another. I saw Waterworth, the policeman, come to the window opposite mine and look about and I, of course, went to my window. The crackling still continued – under our feet it seemed – but nothing could be seen down below in the passage between the buildings. Waterworth ran for his pistol and I put on my coat and went out to the verandah. It was crowded, but the shooting remained unexplained. We looked over the verandah. There were crowds on the other side of the street gazing at Writer's Buildings – but no excitement. The crackling appeared to be further along.

I rushed along but still nothing was visible. The noise seemed to come from the foundations of the building. All the secretaries were out and the place swarmed with *chaprassis*. But no one knew what was happening. One of the Members said he smelt powder. We looked at the street – the crowd was still orderly and gazing at the offices, but traffic was passing by. There was another spurt of crackling still further on. I went along. It was uncanny hearing the noise of shooting yet being unable to locate where it came from. I had heard that there had been trouble at Lal Bazaar, the police station just a stone's throw away on the other side of the church. Again a spurt of crackling and – silence.

We looked into the courtyards at the back and everything was quiet, but there were crowds moving about in the passages. Then I heard that the Inspector General had been shot and the doors of the second story closed and, seeing a surging mass of peons and others at a back stairway, I went down it and looked through the window where I saw the I.G. of Prisons lying in a pool of blood. I passed on quickly, I can tell you, and came on to the second story, which was packed. No one could rightly say what had happened, or whether the murderers had been shot.

Philpot was standing by his office and said he had heard the shots, but thought they came from crackers, and the Government Solicitor saw the men dash out of the I.G.'s room, two of them brandishing revolvers and shooting into the doors along the passage. He could hardly realise what was happening. Col. Simpson's room was very close to mine although on a lower floor. There were crowds of *chaprassis* trying to see the Colonel's body, but no one heeded them. A rumour got about that the murderers were still at large in the building.

We stood about and talked, and then word was passed along that the younger Nelson was hit. I had been speaking to his brother after I came down, and he did not seem to know then. However, when I saw him coming down the verandah he told me that his brother had been hit through the leg, but it was not serious. The Nelson brother who was not shot was staying in the same house as Col. Simpson.

The firing had stopped for some time, and people were passing up and down the verandah. Further along I met Townend, whose office was on the second floor. The youths had rushed into his room and fired; he had lifted a chair and a bullet had ricocheted off and hit him in the back of the neck, cutting his coat but doing no more damage. Nearby a flower pot was overturned and a shot was shown in the roof.

In the door of the Finance Members' Room there was a shot hole right through the glass. When the armed youths came into Nelson's room, they had fired and he had tackled them. He had caught one by the hand and turned his revolver on him and pulled the trigger – but the revolver was empty. Another of them hit him on the head and he was shot through the leg. The Sergeants on duty seemed to have come rushing up by this time and, realizing they were trapped, two of the youths seem to have turned their revolvers on themselves and one took cyanide of potassium. This last is dead, but the others are still alive. One of them is said to be the murderer of Loman, the I.G. of Police.

It has been impossible to settle down to anything since. The Club has been a hive of excitement tonight. I won't enlarge on what has been said, but the murder of a man like Simpson arouses the worst in one. As Inspector of Police he was, if anything, too gentle and generous, and I believe fell into the bad graces of Government for being too forgiving. Yet it is he the swine shot. It is sickening, and makes one full of hate for the brutes.

It is bad enough to have been so close to it all – I have told you the facts and they are sufficient. When the shooting was on I felt perfectly collected – but now I have a hell of a head. Writing has done it good. Don't worry please at the news. We shall all be careful and the offices will be well guarded.

9.12.30

Just returned from the funeral of the I.G. at the Military Cemetery. It was a vast place full of old graves. Few of us had ever been, hidden as it is from the main roads. The service was short and with full military honours – but one had to wait about three quarters of an hour. Even while the cortege was nearing the grave we could hear a band in the distance playing gay airs – and during the service men rushed about with cameras to secure press photos.

Waiting, I heard more stories about what had occurred and how fortunate had been the escape of so many of the officials. Also, that the murderers' nerve seemed to have gone after killing the Colonel, or they might have done more damage. Nelson was going to his door to look out, thinking as we all did that something was up in the street. He was shot at and hit in the leg. His assailant then shot him again but missed. Nelson thought he might as well fight and tackled the man, caught his wrist and turned his revolver on him but, pulling the trigger, found the shot exhausted. His assailant called to his friends for help. They rushed in but seem also to have been without ammunition, for they hit Nelson on the head with the butts of their revolvers. Nelson let go and struggled out of the room. The Police came up and trapped the murderers in Nelson's room, when they attempted to commit suicide. One shot himself through the chin and the bullet penetrated his skull. He is still alive. The other shot himself through the head and he too is still alive.

10.12.30

Today Writer's Building is well guarded. The staircase I used is closed.

The main staircase is set apart for officers, and the west staircase is for the general public. Also, the railings at the back are being bricked up. The Police, with European sergeants, are on guard on all floors. I don't suppose any revolutionary would come, even without these precautions being taken. Their next appearance will be in some place where no one ever expects them.

12.12.30
I shall get to bed early for once, so cheerio. Heaps of love and, if this comes before Xmas, I hope you all have a very Merry Christmas.

The Santals
The Santals were aboriginals who lived in the district of the borderlands with Bihar. They were poor and neglected, but always seemed to be happy. They had one failing in the eyes of the Hindus and Moslems – they loved drink. It was not a very sophisticated drink, but a rice beer, which was home-brewed. They could get a licence for a brewing, but they were poor and licences were not always readily granted so, as often as not, they brewed without the licence. If caught, they would be prosecuted and fined. Usually it was the women who were the brewers, while the men went out to work.

One year there was some scarcity, and prices were high and, when one of the members of the Executive Council went to inspect the jail at Midnapur, he found the women's wards full of Santal women, each with one or more infants. The ward was like a large nursery. The women did not mind being there, for times were hard, and they were getting

Santal dancers

good meals, which they could not have afforded for themselves and their many offspring. That could not be allowed to continue so, as Excise Commissioner (1935-42), I arranged that licences be easily obtainable, and at reasonable rates, and that those who did brew illicitly could compound their offence without being dragged to Court or going to jail. This also helped the Courts by relieving them of these very petty cases.

1921: An unsavoury meal in Khetlal

The Barinal in Bogra, with its *khujar* soil can, in the months before the monsoon, be one of the hottest parts of Bengal with temperatures soaring to 110°, so I was not surprised when I was in Khetlal, which is in the heart of Barinal and miles from any railway station, that the chicken I was served for dinner was not at its freshest. It was not bad but, as one says of milk, 'on the turn'. I was, however, annoyed when the chicken that I had for breakfast at about 7.00 a.m. – my sole meal till the late evening – was definitely so 'off' as to be quite inedible. I called the servant and demanded to know why I had been given rotten food, but I was told that the bird had been killed at 3.00 a.m., and it could not have been bad. It was the ghee which was bad. It had been bought in Khetlal the previous night. I took a sample of the ghee and, along with all the files and papers which had been sent for my attention from the Settlement Office in Bogra, I sent it to the District Magistrate in Bogra with a letter suggesting that some action should be taken against the shopkeeper, as his ghee was dangerous to health.

A month later I had to come back to Khetlal for further inspection. The locals soon told me how the shopkeeper, after receiving a notice from the District Magistrate, had tried to make a personal appeal to me, and had gone first to one place where he heard I was, then to another and another, only to learn that I had gone elsewhere. At last he had attended the Court in Bogra, had pleaded guilty and promised never to offend again: and his plea had been accepted, I suppose because he had already been put to great trouble. The locals, however, had been told the reason why he had been summoned to Bogra and said, 'You see what sort of ghee we have had to put up with.' Then he came to me, and said he was sorry for what had happened and that if only he had known that the ghee was for me, he would not have sold it to my servants. I think he had learned his lesson and, at any rate, the villagers knew what to do if he slipped back into his old habits and started to serve inferior ghee. I had to visit Khetlal on several later occasions, and I never heard any complaints about the quality of the ghee.

1920: A strident woman

Not all women in Bengal were downtrodden helpless creatures. Some of them, especially in the villages, could give a very good account of themselves. One afternoon, when I was returning from a tour of inspection in the fields, the road I was following suddenly came to an end and two smaller roads (just dirt tracks) branched off it westwards. One would take me to the Dak Bungalow where I had my camp in ten minutes or a quarter of an hour, while the other would lead me into unknown land, and perhaps hostile villages, for the troubles in Bogra had only subsided a week or so previously and there were places where an official was still treated as an enemy. Signposts were only found on the few main roads of the district, and I just did not know which road I should take. Then I heard the voice of a woman – in anger. Words poured forth in an ever-increasing stream and an exceptional variety. Once she had started, her voice became louder and shriller. There was no chance of stopping her eloquence. Whoever it was she was addressing could not get a word in as justification. When, at last, she had to take breath for a moment, I managed to shout so that I could be heard during the respite from the din. A small weary man appeared from the hut. I asked for the direction to the Dak Bungalow and, when he replied, I thanked him for his help, and wondered if he would tell me what was the reason for all the row I had heard.

His wife wanted a new cloth and, when he had gone to the 'hut' market, which was some five or six miles off, he had bought her a cloth which he thought she would like. It had not been what she wanted. She would have a cloth like that of one of her neighbours, and no other cloth would do. She ordered him to return at once to the market and change the cloth, but he said he could not do that. Though it was still afternoon, the shadows were lengthening and, by the time he reached the market, all the stall holders would have gone, and it would be dark. Certainly, before he left, some of the stall holders had begun to pack. But she would not listen. No matter what he said, she kept on telling him that he had to go and go at once, and that on no account would she ever wear the cloth he had bought. What advice could I give him? He was only speaking the truth. The market would have been over by the time he reached it, and none of those villagers ever liked walking the roads by night. I told him to say that I had agreed that the market would be over and that it was useless for him to go

160

there, and perhaps she would see reason. As I rode away, I did not hear a recurrence of her shrill voice. Perhaps she had listened after all.

1927: Khulna

Khulna was a delightful spot and I used to watch the sun rise over the junction of two streams of the Delta from my verandah as I had my *polin ka cha* my morning tea. The touring was by river launch through the Sunderbuns (where I could hear the tigers roar though I never saw one), and as far as the sands of the Bay of Bengal, where one can be the only visitor. Khulna was a backwater, and it was just to enliven the place that I suggested there should be an exhibition, with a show of Arts & Crafts from the various Social Departments of Government, such as Health, Agriculture, etc.

I had no idea that it would be taken up so enthusiastically, or that my idea that there should be a Purdah Day – Women Only – would meet with such approval. By British standards it was a very poor affair, and quite small, but it was the first there had been, and that was something. We had some pictures from the Calcutta School of Art, and a few paintings from a local Art School, which were dreadful but highly appreciated because they were local. There were carvings from Madras (I bought a sandalwood handkerchief box for £2 – no bargaining). There was some weaving and the displays from the Government Departments were quite impressive and effective, I

The house at Khulna

161

believe, in putting over their message. Perhaps the most interesting exhibit of all was a live python. Where it had come from I never knew, but it attracted a great attention. Oh, and there was a man who came from Nadia who could transform a lump of clay into a human likeness. He was good, but all his figures had Indian features. There was one of me, which all the Government people said was me to a T. However, when she saw it Marie, my wife, asked who the Bengali was!

Though this exhibition was not advertised in the local press, everybody in the district heard of it, and families came from remote parts. One party of women came from Sutkhain – with approved male escort – which meant they had to travel all day on one of the river steamers, so that the return journey to see the exhibition took three days.

I was pleased that the exhibition was so successful. I visited several times to ascertain how well it was being patronized, and was satisfied with what I saw. But it was the Women's Day which surpassed them all. From the time it opened, it was packed and packed it remained all day. I had to take this on trust, but I could see the box gharries driving up to the entrance to discharge their female cargo. Never did the gharri wallahs have such a profitable day. They were busy from morning to night. The Exhibition was timed to close at 6.00 p.m. but well over an hour later there were still crowds of women going round to make certain

Khulna Recreation Club members

they had not missed anything. The last women did not leave that Exhibition until well after 8.00.

After such a triumphant success it was not to be wondered at that everybody in this district was in an open and friendly mood for a week or two to come, and the Sports Committee showed some true *esprit de corps*.

Of course, ordinarily, the man in the house did all the marketing for his womenfolk – as was brought home to me in Khulna. The Town Sports Committee had to meet one Saturday morning to try to bring some sort of peace amongst the Muslims. They always talked of the Sporting Spirit and *esprit de corps*, but incessantly intrigued amongst themselves in a most unsportsmanlike fashion. In the absence of the Vice-Chairman, the meeting could not begin, much as I as Chairman would have liked it, because the Vice-Chairman was most deeply involved in the row which threatened the very existence of this Committee.

At length, after fully three quarters of an hour had passed, the Vice-Chairman arrived panting and out of breath. He was probably the most promising of the younger members of the local Bar and prided himself on his modern vices and outlooks. He excused himself because he had had to go to the Exhibition which closed on the Friday, to persuade some of the exhibitors to take back some of the clothes his wife had purchased the previous day – a Purdah Day. He must have had some success in persuading the merchants to meet at least most of his demands because he was in a very conciliatory mood, and the meeting proceeded in an unusually amicable way. All the other members were equally disposed to put a rein on their demands and adopt, as they would say, a *via media*. Everyone was pleased that the first exhibition in the town had proved so popular, especially with the women on the Purdah Day, so it proved how progressive the place was. Today, I believe, Khulna is quite a busy river port, with a thriving trade in prawns, which I never tasted all the time I was there.

Two memorable journeys

I have described in perhaps undue length the discomforts of some of the journeys by rail that I took while in India, but I cannot omit an account of two other journeys, one by rail, which were memorable.

I have, on occasion, scoffed at these packaged holidays for a week or a fortnight in far away places such as Australia and Hong Kong, when so much time is spent on the flights, to say nothing of the jet-lag for the few days in the Orient or Down Under, but I forget that when I went for my first visit to Darjeeling from Chittagong in 1919, the journey by rail and steamer took about forty hours for the eight days of the Pujah holidays and there were five changes *en route*. A similar time was spent on the journey back. Everybody seemed to do it and when the little train from Siliguri turned a corner as it zig-zagged up the steep ascent of 6,000 feet to Darjeeling, one might consider the first wonder at the view of the Kanchenjunga Range well worth the weariness of the days in the train, but it was for another reason that I recall this journey.

1919: I left Chittagong at about 10.00 p.m. on a Saturday. John Steven, of the PWD, was a fellow traveller, but not all the way. At 4.00 a.m. he transferred to the steamer at Chandpur. It was dark, and there were rumours of a terrible storm – but nobody could tell us anything definite. As soon as light dawned, we could see the havoc which the storm had wreaked. Boats had been blown from the river on to the tops of houses. Roofs had been blown off, and many of the small huts had collapsed. There was devastation everywhere. Swollen bodies of cattle were floating down the stream, and crows were picking at the eyes of the dead beasts. Hour after hour we passed through such scenes. The crowds at the Ghats seemed half dazed by what they had gone through. One sees the debris of such cyclones on TV, but one cannot grasp the full enormity of the devastation and the sheer helplessness of humanity at such disasters, which are beyond their control. I have never seen the effects of another cyclone.

The bearer I had at that time was a Moslem from the Dacca District and, as the steamer passed village after ruined village, he became more and more worried because his home was somewhere in that area. He helped me transfer my luggage at Godasvo, and asked if I would let him return to see whether his family and his house were safe. I could not refuse, though it meant I should have to be my own valet in the Hills.

There was a short rail journey to Khastia, where we had to wait in an unprotected station for two hours until the Darjeeling Mail arrived. It took us as far as Santaker, where we had a break then transferred with sleepers on the metric gauge line to Siliguri where we had breakfast before joining the toy train that took us up the hill, but with a stop of about an hour at Kurseong for a bite of lunch, before completing the final run to Darjeeling.

When I returned to Chittagong after the Pujahs, the most obvious damage of the storm had been cleared away and, when I went about a month later from Chittagong to Calcutta for my Departmental Examinations, I would hardly have known that there had been a cyclone only two months previously.

1934: At some time or other, there must have been a reason for the inclusion of the subdivision of Arambagh in the Hooghly-Chinsurah District, but nobody knew what it was or could imagine how anyone could have thought it would be a workable arrangement. Arambagh was entirely different in character from the other parts of the district and, in addition, was cut off from them by the River Davodan, which for months on end could not be crossed. Even when the water was low, the crossing was a very rough ride and not suitable for motor vehicles. Arambagh, therefore, was the unvisited Sub-Division, and the people felt they were abandoned, because they were backward, poor and left out of all Government largesse. I had received one or two reminders that I ought to include an inspection of Arambagh during my winter touring, and when I told Marie, my wife, of my intention to comply with these suggestions, she said she would accompany me. Nothing I could say convinced her that the going would be hard – and I had to make plans which I believed left nothing to chance. I'd go to Burdwan, have the car there in the DM's stables, cross the river by elephant, by grace of the Rajkumar, and have a taxi waiting on the other bank to take us the sixteen or so miles to the little town.

The first stage of the journey passed without incident. We made Burdwan in good time, and the DM, Mike Stewart, asked us to lunch in the bungalow I knew so well. I remember he said how grateful they were for the hedge of limes I had planted some four years before. (The plants were supplied gratis by the Botanic Gardens, so I had nothing to pay.) If you wanted a lime drink, a servant was told to go and pick one, and there always seemed to be limes to pick. We had almost finished lunch when the house shook, and when there was another tremor we ran outside and kept at a distance from the house. Mike ran upstairs to bring his two children down. There was a feeling of fear and expectancy in the air. There was not a sound to be heard; there was no movement of the leaves in the great lychee trees in the garden, and the waters in the pond were see-sawing, with the surface as rigid as that of a billiard table. It was so uncanny; one did not want to speak: one just waited. Suddenly the tremors ceased and, just as suddenly,

165

everything came alive again. The birds began to sing, and there was a rustle in the leaves. We returned to the house and sat for a short time with the Stewarts, before leaving to complete our journey: but we had no heart for talk.

We arrived at the crossing and found the elephant waiting, and were surprised to hear of some other sahibs who had crossed a short time before we came. We could not imagine who they could be. We were soon mounted and seated on the mattress strapped to the elephant's back, not comfortably and, as it slithered down the sandy bank of the river, very precariously we thought. The month was January and the water in the river was at its lowest, leaving a long stretch of sand, which we would have found most awkward to traverse, but which the elephant managed with ease.

When we had dismounted and looked around for the taxi, there was not a vehicle to be seen, and the order for the taxi to be there had been specific. I went to some huts and asked where the taxi could be, and was told there had been a taxi, but some sahibs had come along and had ordered the driver to take them to Arambagh. They had left not so very long before our arrival. We could not go back to Burdwan – the elephant had gone – and we just had to wait hopefully. There could be no more unsuitable spot. There was no shade and, though it was the cold weather, the sand seemed to radiate heat. Not till long past our normal tea-time did the taxi return from Arambagh. He said he had

Crossing river by elephant

166

not been told who was coming and, when the sahibs arrived, he accepted what they said and drove off with them. It was the usual Mofussal taxi, of great age and much repaired. The road was bumpy, so the journey to Arambagh – which in Urdu means the Garden of Rest (Leisure not Death) – was neither fast nor comfortable. We heard that the sahib who had taken the taxi was from Chinsurah, and I think he need not have been so precipitate. I do not know where he lodged for the night. That was my wife's first experience of accompanying me on tour, and it discouraged her from wanting to join me when on inspection as long as we were in Hooghly.

1921-1922: Death in the Waiting Room

There was an old Scots saying, I believe, that if you met a funeral after setting out from home you should turn around and go back home to base: to proceed was to journey into trouble. I did not meet a funeral – it was a death! I could not go back, and it was trouble that was in store for me.

In the first year of the Settlement I had been stationed during all the hot weather in Patna. I was in charge of the surveying of the land and the preliminary recording of the villages of what was called the Sadar Sub-Division of the District. With the advent of the cooler months, a move was to be made to Bogra for the survey etc. of that district. Bogra nowadays boasts an airport. Then it was a District without the ordinary facilities, and no accommodation for European Officers except the Circuit House, where one's occupancy was precarious and uncomfortable.

The population of the Sadar Sub-Division was mixed and, though occasional agitation did cause annoyance, generally no opposition was encountered. For some decades the population had been falling, and there existed an air of lassitude, possibly the legacy of malaria. Bogra, however, was nearly 90 per cent Moslem, and the people were energetic and far less placid. They may have listened to the men of the Congress but as these were always or nearly always Hindus, they were little influenced by what they heard. They feared the Hindu power. Events in the West caused them great concern when, in the peace-making after the 1914-18 War, the Sultan of Turkey was de-throned and Turkey declared a Republic. The Sultan was no longer the Khalifa, and the cry that Mohammedanism was in danger aroused a passionate hatred against Britain (one of the Peace-making Powers), which inflamed every Moslem peasant.

We heard in Patna that the *amins* (the surveyors) who were assembling in Bogra were being boycotted and resisted when they went to secure accommodation and food. Prospects for work in the second season were bleak. Patna and Bogra might be neighbouring Districts, but communication between them was negligible, and was not assisted by the lack of any direct through roads. Firstly one had to get to Ishurdi, the railway junction at the end of the bridge over the Ganges. There was a dirt-track road of sorts, on which a bus plied intermittently, and there was a small river steamer, which was more comfortable, though one had to be able to climb from the Ghat up the embankment to the station. Its timing did not always synchronize with the timing of the Mails on the main line, so one generally had quite a long spell to spend at the station waiting for the connection. Then one took a fast train to Santahar, which was then the junction where all changed for the night journey to Darjeeling by the metric gauge sleepers. It was also the junction for Bogra, twenty seven miles away. I got to know these two junctions very well – their waiting rooms and their refreshment or dining saloons.

My servants may have been reluctant to go to Bogra. They made so much bother and delay about getting everything ready that I was detained, and exasperated. However, they did manage to catch the bus and the trains as planned. I took the steamer, but it was late in reaching the junction, and I was faced with five or six hours to spend in the waiting room before the train arrived at about 2.30 a.m. The meal was just fodder, and no more, but for fodder I had to be grateful. I had no book or magazine with me, and there was nothing readable to purchase, so I only had to count the hours in the waiting room, which was very dimly lit. I did amuse myself by inspecting the stock in the sales cabinet in the refreshment room. Some of the toiletries seem to have been left over from the nineteenth century, when Ishurdi was quite an important changing post. I wish I had bought one or two, to preserve the literature that went with the packaging, with its obviously fictitious personages fulsomely recommending the article and the testimonials of several of the Dukes who were sons of George III, and are now forgotten.

When all that paled, I stretched out on one of the chairs with supports for the legs – I think they are called 'Planters' Chairs' – and had a very broken nap, because of the goods trains rattling through the station just when I was about to fall into restful slumber. Then, at about 12.00, the door to the waiting room opened. They were obviously minor railway officials, one from Khurai and the other from Calcutta. They exchanged a few words, said goodbye, and the local man went away. The door clanged as he departed. The other one stood for about a minute or so, went to the other chair, and then dropped dead into it. He passed out without a murmur. There was no doubt that he was dead – and it was now midnight. His friend could not be called as he would have left the station, and I had to have the station master roused. As he knew the friend, he arranged to inform the family in Calcutta. What I did afterwards, I am told, was quite beyond such legal powers as I had. I was a Settlement Officer, not a Magistrate, though I had been a Magistrate as Sub-Divisional Officer before that at Sirajganj. However, I was the only eye witness, so I drew up a statement of what happened, and authorized the removal of the body by train to Calcutta. I believe there should have been a formal inquest. There was none, but nobody ever challenged what I had done. I think the staff at Ishurdi station, who were most helpful, thought a very sad situation had been handled most expeditiously and well. At the station I also wrote a letter to the family, giving them an account of the death. It was their due.

I had still an hour or so to wait before the train to Santahar came in. I did manage to have a few hours restless sleep in the compartment which I had to myself. In the morning when I got down from the carriage, I found letters from my last tour blowing about the station platform. I know that the case had been locked before I left Patna but, as it was taken by the servants, it had to be placed in the guard's van. During the night somebody had opened it, but nothing had been taken. Actually, there was nothing that a thief would think worth taking, but it angered me that my case had been tampered with because it was not in my control. It was a very weary exasperated person who arrived later in the morning at Bogra.

Gandhi and the Raj

I shall end with a more heartwarming memory. The time was 1930, when Gandhi was revered in his own land and in many parts as a Saint for his ideal of a Golden Age of non-violent non-co-operation, which almost always ended in bloodshed. It was a time when the intelligentsia in Britain scoffed at the continuance of the Raj, and described their kinsmen in the Government Services as sun-dried bureaucrats, educated in an outworn tradition and out of sympathy with the advancement of the people; when Magistrates and Judges in Bengal, both Indian and British, were targets for the bullets of the terrorists. I was in the grounds of the great marble Memorial to Queen Victoria as Empress of India and saw a poor Indian woman approach the statue of the Queen, and respectfully joining her hands in *pronam*, she stood silently with bowed head a little while before advancing to the statue and laying her forehead reverently on the feet of the Queen. Then she left as unobtrusively as she had come. She was illiterate and one of the lower castes, but probably she represented the majority of the people. Her simple act of gratitude was more typical of their feelings and of their thankfulness for years of peace than the much publicized utterances of the politicians. Often in the flowery language derived from the days of the Moguls, a petitioner seeking redress of some grievance would call the Magistrate *Gharib Parwar* – Protector of the Poor. I like to think that, in their dealings with the peoples of India, the Britons in the service of the Crown were just that. There could be no finer tribute to their work.

Correspondence with the British Museum

In retirement Donald donated a Vishnupatta that he had found to the British Museum 'in memory of his wife and the many happy years in India'. The following letter from the Department of Oriental Antiquities at the British Museum was received by the family after Donald's death.

22nd January, 1990

Dear Miss MacPherson,
Thank you for your kind and full letter of January 5th. I am very sorry to hear your sad news. I greatly admired your late father, welcomed his visits and was, of course, abidingly grateful for his sympathetic generosity to the National Collections, which he enriched with a most interesting gift.

Your letter has saddened me very much and I offer you all my condolences.

May I add a little story? Some years ago, on one of his visits, your father joined a colleague and myself in my office. The colleague was a Bengali and from a part of Bengal where your father had served. Conversation became topographical and we were given an account of that part so detailed and instructive that my colleague, no more than I, could scarcely conceal his amazement. I felt so proud of the old ICS that day.

Thank you again for writing. I am quite sure that I shall remember your father.
Yours very sincerely,

Wladimir Zwalf

THE BRITISH MUSEUM

17 November 1983

Sir,

At their last Meeting the Trustees of the British Museum had before them a report of your most welcome gift in memory of your late wife, Marie E MacPherson, of a stone Vishnupatta from North Bengal.

I am directed by the Trustees to convey to you this expression of their special thanks for your generosity to the Museum.

I have the honour to be,
                         Sir,
            Your obedient Servant

                                    John Wilson

                                    rector

Mr Donald MacPherson CIE MA

Some letters
found among the papers

Alphapore
12.10.40

My dear Sir,
Please accept my Bijoya greetings and the best wishes of the season. May Providence grant you and members of your family health, happiness and prosperity in unbound measure!

It pains me very much to see all that is happening now under the Govt. of Bengal. I quite see from an extract of the *Gazette* what has happened. In recent years no Commissioner of Excise has worked so sincerely and so hard for the improvement of the Excise organisation of the province and no one has succeeded to effect such marvellous improvement in its members as you have done. It is indeed painful to see that powers that be have no eyes to see and appreciate such valuable work.

My old mother, a lady of old school, when she heard of my fate refused to believe it, saying that such injustice was not possible so long as a heir and successor of the late Queen Victoria the Great remained the Emperor of India and ruled over the country. It seems to me as if the British have ceased to exercise their responsibilities, at least so far as Bengal is concerned. As for the rest I and members of my family will be fully prepared to stand trial should an occasion arise in future when our loyalty may be tested.

As regards my petition, I depend entirely on you Sir. Sir, I truly believe that you will very kindly do at the opportune moment what you think to be best for me.
With my best regards,
Yours sincerely,

Ranjit Chowdhury, DSET

Writers Building.
22.8.42

My dear Sir,

Many thanks for your kind letter. I have conveyed your good wishes to all whom I could get hold of in and near about Calcutta, and I shall place the letter before the next Association Meeting. There is absolutely no doubt that your letter will be very much appreciated by all officers and encourage them to emulate the example set by you. As a kind master and well-wisher of the Department you will ever be in the memory of all Excise Officers high or low.

Wishing you and Mrs MacPherson a long life and prosperity and thanking you again for your very kind letter, I remain,
Yours sincerely,

B. Suliman.

Raja Sita Ram Road.
21.8.42

My dear Sir,
I could not feel what was happening the other night until the
train steamed out of the platform and the sorrow became greater
and greater in office yesterday every time I went to answer a
telephone call to say that you were transferred as Divisional
Commissioner Rajstahi and had left Calcutta. You, Sir, left a
void in our hearts which will never he filled. The demonstration
at the Sealdah station, spontaneous as it was, is the proof positive
of the sincerity of these words.

I hope that you had a convenient journey and arrived safely
at Jalpaiguri. We have as yet no information about the movement
of our successor. Baghur Ruham is only doing his routine duties.
Kindly tender my respectful compliments and regards to Mrs
MacPherson. We are all so sorry that we did not get an
opportunity to pay our respects to her as she was not in Calcutta.

Ever praying for the very best of luck to you and yours and
with my best regards, I remain,
Yours sincerely,

Ranjit

Sir,

I beg to lay the following history for your information requesting advice to the matter as stated hereafter.

A rabid dog after biting several cattle and child bate a domesticated gander to bloodshed i.e. blood discharged from the sore (made by biting of the dog) of the gander. The gander after some 3 days i.e. within the week of its being bitten knocked some child and adult of the family with his beak as he was accustomed to do since before, but no bloodshed from the knocking of the gander. Moreover the gander used to drink water some-times from the water cans, and feed himself from the stock of provision such as rice of the family as he was accustomed to do always since he had been domesticated. The gander, however, has been cleared off from the family in its normal condition, on the supposition that it may turn rabid and do harm to the family in the long run. Under the circumstances related above, I shall be much obliged if you would kindly let me know if the members of the family (knocked by the gander) may be contaged with the poison or germ of Hydrofobea and should they be treated therefore.

An early reply will highly oblige.
Yours faithfully

To The Director, Pasteur Institute, Shillong.   No date given

Sir,

I beg most respectfully to approach you with the following in expectation that you will kindly oblige me with your advice so that I may act upon it and free myself from anxiety as I am now in.

Some six months ago, say on the month of March 1917, I was bitten by an old cat on the lower part of my right leg. The cat struck me on the right part of the leg near the hill, making two deep wounds from which blood run out excessively. I at once run to a Physician with whose advice I applied caustic lotion. I do not distinctly remember what. It took a few days to recover myself from the wounds which was widen after the application of the lotion. The wounds were made by the teeth and nails of the cat. From that time I am becoming weak day after day and am afraid that some sort of poison is work within my system, which is telling on my vitality. My health has been broken down – complexion going to be pale – loosing appetite and digestive power. The cat was old and probably attacked with some sort of disease. It used to bask in the sun just near the front of my room. Accidentally I put my feet upon it and it grew furious and struck me. Now I invite your careful consideration to the matter and beg to know whether it will be necessary for me to come to you for the treatment or whether any sort of treatment is necessary for the bite of a cat which was old and ill.

I am aged about 25 years and was in youthful bloom before that time. I shall be glad to furnish you with any sorts of particulars if required.